INSIDER'S SECRETS TO FLIPPING HOUSES FOR MASSIVE PROFITS

THE ULTIMATE GUIDE TO MAKING REAL MONEY AND REHABBING HOUSES THE RIGHT WAY

By Michael Mireiter

Publisher's Note:

Copyright 2019 - Legacy Publishing LLC
All Rights Reserved

ISBN - 978-1-7342999-0-8

ISBN 978-1-7342999-0-8

9 781734 299908 >

Cover design, internal formatting & layout: Hemant Lal
www.AaronProductionsIndia.com

FOREWORD

Dear Reader,

I've been doing real estate now for more than 23 years, and it's an understatement to say that I've met a LOT of people. Some were clients, some were vendors, some were students I mentored. And here's what I've learned over the years: There are many people who say they're going to do something...but not so many who actually follow through and do what they say.

Lots of talk...not so much walk.

But the author of this book is someone who walks the talk. He says what he's going to do...and then he actually goes out and does it. That's true in the little things and the big things, as I'm about to share.

I first met Mike not through real estate but when I needed some trees at my Ohio house. I was a customer looking for a service, and Mike was referred to me by the company I bought the trees from.

Mike owned a landscaping company. I called him, and he said he'd be there at 1:00 p.m.

"Sure," I thought to myself. "We'll see about that." In my years of working with people, I'd often come to doubt that kind of appointment-setting. Truth be told, I expected him to show up between 3:30 and 5:30 or even the next day. (If you've ever tried to hire a trade to come to your house, you know this is not normal.)

But sure enough, at 1:00 p.m. sharp, I saw him pull up! (Now, it almost sounds silly to write that, but I've learned that doing what you say and keeping your word are rare qualities in a person.)

I was impressed by his commitment, follow-through, and integrity. I was so impressed, in fact, that I hired his company a lot over the next 12 months. Every single time, he showed up on time, he did the work on time, and his work was on budget. (Again, that's not normal for this line of work.)

So we started talking more and more. Before you know it, we were doing deals, and I watched him accelerate the success… all thanks to the simple "secret" of showing up and doing what he said he was going to do.

I love seeing quality people win at BIG levels.

I've seen Mike turn ugly houses into amazing homes for families…all in a very quick timeline.

I know he's just getting started, and I'm glad to not only call him a great investor but a friend.

So here's my recommendation: Take this book and read each page. Highlight as you go, and learn from the lessons in it… then go out and do what he teaches! Before you know it, you can be sitting on an amazing portfolio of deals that you've created.

I do know real estate is an amazing asset and can accomplish any dream one has in life with the right approach and work ethic, and Mike has both! So dig in and enjoy the ride.

Onward and upward,

Mark Evans, DM
Nine-time best-selling author, investor, and business owner

DEDICATION

There are two things you should know about my dad. He was always my biggest advocate, and he always did things the right way. I saw that when we remodeled our kitchen and bathrooms and completely finished the basement in the house where I grew up. Watching my dad work—and having him as a teacher—inspired me to explore a career in construction when I was older. Along the way, Dad has always been there for me, no matter how crazy the endeavor sounded.

It may be hard to believe, but when I was only 15 years old, I decided I wanted to start a hard-surface countertop company. No problem, right? I called Corian, the material manufacturer, and scheduled an appointment with their regional representative. When my father heard my plan, he didn't shoot down the meeting. Instead, he went with me.

We met with the Corian representative on a cold, February morning at a McDonald's restaurant. As we sat down with the rep (remember, I wasn't even old enough to drive), I was as sure as the sun and the moon that not only was this a reasonable career move but it was absolutely what I wanted to do with my life. Clearly, the rep was surprised to see a teenager at the meeting, but he took the time to explain the entire process involved in acquiring a dealership. Dad sat through the whole meeting with me, asking a few questions but letting me do the lion's share of the talking.

Throughout the meeting and then when it was time to make an actual decision, my father never told me that I was attempting the impossible or that I was too young for such a huge and costly business venture. Instead, like he'd done in countless building and repair projects, he did things the right way. He respected my independence and told me he would support me, whatever the decision. While I ultimately decided against the deal, that experience stays in my head and my heart to this day.

This book is dedicated to my father, who taught me to love working with my hands and to appreciate the craft of construction. He has always been there to help me, to support my ideas (no matter how wild they may be), and to walk beside me on the journey.

Thank you, Dad.

PREFACE

Real estate investing can be incredibly profitable and can offer many rewards. As I've continually learned, how well it works for you will often come down to exactly how you do it.

Presently, I flip multiple houses every month. Throughout this book, I will identify and describe some of the best practices to get the results you really want most from real estate and how to avoid the pitfalls that can break you.

Table of Contents

INTRODUCTION

Forget what you've seen on TV. This book is about what flipping real estate looks like in real life, the mistakes to avoid, and what it takes to actually get paid well while fully enjoying what you do.

"If you love what you do, you will never work a day in your life." —Unknown

Within these pages, you will find my personal story of getting started in real estate investing. You will read about the detours I took to get where I am today, the misconceptions I had to break through to get here, and the satisfaction of turning tough deals into real dollars.

Read on if you are looking to break into real estate with more reliable profits by using proven processes your team can start plugging into immediately. If you have found yourself stuck in the process of flipping, if you are busy flipping but have hit a plateau, if you are not realizing the results from flipping that you expected, or if you are already doing a good number of deals but want to flip more, then this book is for you.

ABOUT THE AUTHOR

Hi! I'm Michael Mireiter, just an average guy who grew up in the Midwest and someone who always felt there was something more out there. I grew up knowing deep down inside that there was a better way to earn an incredible income and enjoy making a living in a way that would also be valuable to others.

Fast forward many years, and I've founded several businesses. But in the end, over time, I found that real estate was the ultimate shortcut for making a great income while gaining more control over my time and being able to do something I'm really proud of every single day.

Having said that, I have not always nailed it the first time around. I've found myself involved in some ugly deals that left me with some very tough decisions to make. I've been through a lot of trial and error over the years in order to develop and perfect a great flipping system that really works every time.

For me, that means being able to leverage a predictable process and, in doing so, control the outcomes of the real estate deals in which I invest. I am still flipping houses every day, though now it is more for the pleasure of seeing the finished product and the joy it brings to the end buyers than for the need to generate income.

I am not a gifted real estate flipping phenom. I am just an average but active real estate investor who has done things the hard way and thereby learned how to make house flipping easier along the way.

Hopefully, this book will help speed up your journey of flipping real estate with fewer mistakes and more great wins.

You can also check out my personal website (MikeMireiter.com) for more resources, real estate forms, and a way to ask me questions if you're stuck on a deal.

Happy Reading!
Michael Mireiter

WHAT THIS INFORMATION HAS DONE FOR ME

The information on these pages is comprised of many of the tools, processes, and systems I use to run my real estate flipping business today. They are the resources I am using now to create consistent wins when flipping houses.

These tools have allowed me a greater personal freedom than most people think is possible. They help me avoid major financial obstacles, and they allow me to make a positive difference for many families and communities. As an added bonus, I get to spend a lot more time with my own family.

Looking back on my journey through the process of writing and publishing this book, I've been reminded of a lot of good lessons I've learned along the way—what works and what doesn't and the factors that drove the improvements. Using those lessons, I have been able to identify and perfect each step in my flipping system, and I am now going to share them with you.

In this book, you'll find the following:

- How to avoid taking the long route to success
- What it takes to make REAL money in real estate
- How I inspect and value properties
- My 10-step process to rehabbing retail houses
- Finding the money to get started or up your game
- Where to find the deals
- How to overcome getting stuck
- How to get to the next level if already investing

What This Book Can (and Won't) Do for You

There are no get-rich-quick schemes inside this book. But it will show you how to change the dynamics of your finances and lifestyle through real estate. To do so successfully, however, requires you to pay attention to the details, to put in the work, and to invest in yourself.

This book WILL NOT show you how to cheat the system or take shortcuts that will land you in jail after a short stint of success.

This book WILL show you:

- How you can get started flipping houses, even without many resources.
- How to get funded for deals.
- How to side-step common traps that will keep you broke or bankrupt you.
- What it takes to renovate and flip houses every month.
- The 3 C's it takes to succeed.

Chapter 1

Drive and Take the Scenic Route

Why did I have to create four separate companies to realize where I wanted to go in life?

I've never been afraid of hard work. In fact, I've always been quite entrepreneurial. Through it all, I've discovered that there is a lot more to running a truly profitable business that gives you all the great rewards of being your own boss than you might see on the surface.

Like I said, I've started several businesses. While they may have been better than working for someone else, they didn't always give me the surplus disposable income or personal freedom you'd imagine from being the CEO of your own company.

This book will help you avoid some of the many detours I have already travelled so you can get right where you want to be and save years of learning in the process.

Always Driven

Growing up, I always possessed drive, ambition, and a seemingly endless supply of creativity.

I am not sure if you can succeed without those three things. With them, I am sure you can do anything. If you research the biographies of any highly successful investor or business leader—or even charitable philanthropists—you will find those three ingredients in their personalities.

Of course, drive alone doesn't guarantee a fast and direct path to success. While having some hustle is good, you can sprint in the wrong direction and not get where you want to go at all.

Today, I believe that the more we learn from others, the more direct the path to success will be (and with a lot less risk). I have heard it said (and allow me to paraphrase) that a smart person learns from their own mistakes, but a wise person learns from other people's mistakes so they don't have to make them. This is the ultimate truth.

If you stay driven, learn to be coachable, are willing to learn new ways of doing things, find great people to learn from, and then put in the work on the process you have learned, that's when the magic happens.

The Start of the Journey

I was born in a very rural area before moving to the suburbs of Cleveland, Ohio.

In my school years, I was always very focused on trying to get work and create money from doing odd jobs around the community. I was very engaged in watching my dad do remodeling projects around the house. I would help him anytime he was working on one of those projects.

My dad always did things the right way. Together, we remodeled our kitchen and two bathrooms and then completely finished the basement. I learned quickly that I wanted to grow up and become involved in the construction industry in some fashion.

Throughout my middle school education, I was never inspired by trying to make good grades. I was not interested in completing my homework and doing all the classroom assignments the teacher expected from me.

When I got to high school, I decided to make a mindset shift. I didn't want to be held back a grade or otherwise not complete high school on time. That big fear compelled me to take my high school education very seriously. I started using any extra time I had in school to work on my homework. I studied for tests during school hours, and I became very efficient using my time. Once I shifted my mindset toward being more proactive and productive, it opened up a lot of doors and allowed me to accomplish so much more.

I got my grades up. However, my deep-down drive was still getting into the outdoors and making money.

Chapter 2

My First Company

I started a construction company during my senior year in high school. Although I didn't have the experience to know how to run a business properly, I had been in the construction trades vocational program for two years. It was after high school that construction became my full-time passion.

I was the guy who would run my estimates in the evening or at lunchtime. The rest of my time was consumed by swinging a hammer 12 to 14 hours a day. There was no team behind me. I was running aimlessly through my days. Busy, busy, busy. I was back in my elementary and middle school way of thinking. There was no focus.

Sure, I was creating a paycheck and was able to support myself. There just wasn't a lot of income left over to be able to do the things I wanted to (and some things I needed to do).

The mindset I was following was to be able to put things off and that things would be different so I would have more free time and money. As you gain these experiences, you grow and come to realize that there are some things you really can't afford to gamble on with your future. The dynamics of your finances and your time are not going to change unless you change what you are doing right now.

Owning a business and working very long hours left me feeling entitled to extra money. I imagined that more free income would just appear after the next job or the next month. Maybe after the next tax season, things would really be different. Maybe next year, that will be it. Of course, things never change. Not until you do.

Chapter 3

MINDSET SHIFT

None of those lies I was telling myself about my business ever came to pass, and I continued down the wrong path. That can happen as a business owner or in a career you are passionate about while working for someone else. It can even happen in real estate and to new investors trying to find their way in the house flipping market.

In my early 20s, I became even more driven. At that time in my life, I set my sights on organizing a company that would create a better financial future for my family and for the team of people working with me.

The truth is that things didn't substantially change until I started investing in myself. Things started happening when I began growing my mindset by actively thinking positively and then taking real action.

There comes a point when you have to say enough is enough. What you are doing isn't working—or at least it isn't going to take you where you want to go—and it's certainly not the way you are doing it right now. Once you draw that line in the sand and get determined to improve, you can find ways to be more efficient with your resources and then work on using the new things that will help you get to the next level.

Myths and Misconceptions

I always had this strange misconception that if there was something in my company that I wasn't really good at, I needed to get excellent at that task or process to be able to drive value for the company.

Often, when you are starting out in business or investing (or even just in your daily life), you think you have to do it all yourself. Some of it is a lack of creativity and resourcefulness. Some of it can be ego.

Through my journey, I found there are certain things I don't want to do. They are things I don't enjoy and things I am just truly not that great at.

One of the best things I was able to learn was that I don't need to be great at everything. It's not necessary to be good at all aspects of everything in your business in order to have a successful company.

The better way you create value for your company is to build a team and an environment where you can utilize the skills of your team without having to do every task or keep all channels of your organization moving through you.

You should be the master of what you are great at. We all have certain strengths, gifts, talents, or experiences that we can keep honing and perfecting to become the best.

Keep working on becoming and remaining the master by using your strengths, gifts, talents, and experiences.

Recognize that the areas in which you are lacking or less passionate don't have to soak up your time. Don't exhaust yourself, drain your energy, and take away from your real strengths by trying to do the things you are less passionate about or talented in.

Once you realize this concept, the value and wisdom of hiring other people who are strong in those things you are less passionate about or talented in can be incredibly freeing. It will also serve to exponentially elevate the potential of your business.

You are not going to get the benefits of a real business owner unless you begin thinking and acting like an entrepreneur instead of having the mindset of a laborer.

That applies to sales, marketing, accounting, customer service, product, and operational processes. The more freely those processes and channels are moving independently without you, the better it is for you and what you are trying to accomplish with your business.

All too often, it is the small business owners who hold themselves back by not letting other people in their organization do the jobs they are less passionate about or talented in. It is not always easy to let go, but doing so will free up large amounts of your time to make better company decisions and create a better financial future for you and your company.

Know that it doesn't always mean you have to take on a lot of overhead for hefty salaries and the risk of in-house employees. It can mean involving mentors, vendors, remote contractors, and freelancers who you just pay as you need them.

Once you free yourself up with a great team, you can spend your time working on your business instead of in your business. Ultimately, one day you want this business to be able to run autonomously on its own while you retire. Or you may want to sell it for even greater wealth to take care of your family.

My message here is to hire the absolute best people you can in every part of your business, inside and out, and get out of their way so they can do their best work.

Doing so allows you to see the 30,000-foot view. You can focus your time on the most important and profitable tasks for your business. You can organize and systemize your business so if one of your vendors or team members has to leave for some reason, someone else can step in easily to keep things moving.

There are many myths and misconceptions about flipping houses and going into the real estate business. We'll cover a few of those later in this book, but if you nail down my recommendation to hire the absolute best people you can in every part of your business, everything else will fall into place.

Processes vs. Progress

As my team and I were working on growing, I started refining and updating our processes and systems.

While processes and systems are essential to have, being sure you are actually making progress personally and in your business is far more important than getting lost in some of the distracting details. You can study my rehabbing process later in this book, but here I want to talk about the bigger picture as an entrepreneur, investor, and leader of your own business.

This "bigger picture process" was essentially me reengaging myself, similar to my high school decisions to constantly improve the use of my time and make concise proactive decisions about getting out of the spinning-my-wheels approach, which left me bouncing around to different goals with little or no focus.

I was determined to forever leave that reactive style approach to business. Indeed, if I kept leading my business down that path, I would either be destined to fail as a company going bankrupt or fail personally, working 14- to 20-hour days trying to keep up and never getting ahead.

Ultimately, I began to consciously buy my time back out of the company. Now, I work toward buying my time back every day.

I look at the issues and problems we face in our day-to-day lives as challenges. I look at who on my team is best fit to handle them. Sometimes, it is still me, but a lot of the time, one of the team members can take the lead on any given challenge. That keeps me free so I can keep my focus on the big-picture items for the company, including growth.

Self-Growth

To continue to grow your investments and your business, you have to keep growing yourself. No one just walks in and becomes the founder of a billion-dollar technology business or a Fortune 500 company. You can't keep doing the same things you did for your first flip if you want to be doing 100 house flips a year. You have to grow. You'll get better with proactively learning new parts of the business, and hopefully, my process will become organic as you keep doing more deals. You also have to grow as a business person, leader, and member of the community in order to achieve your greatest success.

There is a lot I have learned in my 30s that I wish I knew in my 20s.

Leaders Read

One of the best ways to get ahead in learning and self-growth is to always read books and other published works. There are hundreds of business podcasts, YouTube video channels, and real estate blogs to learn from every day. I personally still prefer real books. Whatever you choose, just make sure you are learning from someone who really knows what they are doing and is teaching you responsible techniques to use in your business.

The best way to continually grow personally and stay ahead of how you need to be equipped so your business can grow is to make constant learning a habit. I want to stay on point with rehabbing and flipping in this book, but there are plenty of books out there on growing your mindset and ideas to improve your daily routines. It is amazing how many hours in a day the most successful people spend reading. The more they read, the more successful they seem to become. Just find a time and routine that works for you, and create a daily reading habit.

Mentors and Coaches

Some of the best advice I can give you is to find a trusted mentor and hire a business coach. I have both — a business coach and a few mentors. I love to attend mastermind groups, too. In fact, if it weren't for my mastermind group, I wouldn't have written this book.

There is a huge difference between just piecing together knowledge online and working with a mentor or coach. They have been where you are and can give you real insights you may never find alone. As they say, "It's what you don't know that you don't know that gets you." A mentor and coach can help you see what's ahead, avoid common mistakes, and make helpful suggestions for your business. They can get you on the fast track, show you what's possible, inspire you to achieve, and maybe, most importantly, keep you accountable.

I have found that working with a mentor or business coach really illuminates the self-limiting thoughts we all put upon ourselves. At masterminds, you'll also find others who are on the same journey and may have already found solutions to the challenges you are now facing. By working with a mentor or business coach, maybe you'll gain the capacity to give back to someone else who is a little earlier on their journey than you are now.

One of my favorite things about going to a mastermind event is getting out of my native element and going to a place (physically relocating myself to that new area) for a day or two or three. It helps clear my mind of the day-to-day business thoughts. It frees me from the daily constraints and makes me want to find balance. Go to a mastermind event with an open mindset, and then network and be yourself. I have the most productive week after one of those events and often in the week leading up to it. Going to a mastermind event is making an investment in yourself, and that's the best type of investment you can make.

There are no big successes without mentors or coaches. That applies to real estate and every other type of business or career. Warren Buffett, Tony Robbins, and your favorite athletes have all had mentors and coaches. They often spend more than a million dollars per year to hire them. Keep learning the process, and you'll keep producing more surplus income that you can use to reinvest in yourself. If you can name any athletes with $10 million or more contracts or billionaires who haven't had any coaches or mentors or who don't own real estate, I'd love to hear about them.

I believe in constant improvement as a way of life. I love to attend high-level mastermind events at least three to four times a year to keep up consistent growth. There are plenty of them around the country. Start at whatever level you can and build on that, or you can even start your own. You might also find similar benefits in local real estate clubs and real estate networking events or by attending trade shows and other business events.

You can ask your tax planner for a referral to a good business coach. I usually like to work with people who have a stronger skill set in areas where I don't. Choose one who is active and successful in real estate and has been through some of the experiences you are going through.

You can find mentors in many ways. You may have someone you already know who is getting the types of results and living the type of lifestyle you want. Build on your relationship with them. Some may want money for their time. Some will help with questions for free. Take them to lunch and pick their brains. Some may trade your time or other resources and abilities for their knowledge. Maybe you know how to do the construction part but can partner with them on finding and selling the deals. Maybe you are finding a lot of properties or have the money to invest but could use a second set of eyes from a partner who knows how to manage contractors and how to run an efficient rehab and remarketing campaign.

One thing that is really critical here is that if you are going to invest your time, effort, and money in yourself, make sure you follow through on your commitments. It's great to come out of these events and meetings totally motivated and inspired, but if you don't take action on the insights you have learned or if you don't maintain that energy by participating regularly, all can quickly be lost.

Also, don't try to take on so much at one of these events that you get lost about where to start. Look for one main takeaway from each event. Write it down, commit to action, and keep moving forward toward your goals.

Goal-Setting

Jeff Bezos, the founder of Amazon, has had his fair share of struggles and failures that caused him to almost throw in the towel on his new company. Then he created a business that forever changed the world and consumers' buying habits.

He did not create that overnight. Nor did he create it by measuring his daily activity against his ultimate goals. Yes, your goals should be in line with what you seek daily, but your goals should also rise up to the achievements you desire in the long run.

One of the hardest things I struggled with was putting down my cell phone and taking the time to write down my goals. It may not seem to make sense. It may not sound like a huge difference. Yet there is huge power in writing down your goals. It forces you to think through your plan more decisively and more clearly.

I was always the person who had everything inside my head. It suited me well, but I was never able to achieve anything more than I was immediately doing—that next contracting job, the next flip, the next year, the fluffy and vague five-year goals in my head. It wasn't until I started focusing by identifying and writing down my goals and challenges for a path to success that my path to success really started to happen.

Write Them Down. Be Specific. Read Them Daily.

It's especially helpful if you go really big with your goals and then break them down into chapters of what steps are needed to reach the next milestone on your journey.

You can enrich your morning routine by reading your goals and then following up by reading a chapter a day in a book that's relative to the areas in which you want to improve and make progress. That may even include a book on goals and goal-setting.

Some of my favorite books include:
- *Traction* by Gino Wickman
- *The Ten X* Rule by Grant Cardone
- *The Compound Effect* by Darren Hardy

We Rise by Building Others Up

I don't agree with giving or doing fake things out of a selfish desire to get ahead. Instead, constantly looking for ways to add value for others is essential and probably the most rewarding part of being in real estate.

Helping the people around you create value in their own lives can be accomplished by sharing at mastermind events and networking groups, by writing your own book, or by sharing a great book you've read. Find somebody close to you that you think the book would impact, gift them a copy, and follow up with what they have learned. Find out what their favorite points were, see it from their perspective, and see how they apply it.

Chapter 4

FINDING REAL ESTATE

Real estate investing is something I have been attracted to since I was a teenager. I saw the possibilities of what could be done with a real estate company, and I needed to put a model together so I could do it, too.

Having worked in construction since high school, I got a great understanding of improving properties, what people wanted, and the problems people fell into by not doing proper maintenance or by doing poor repair jobs.

I also saw plenty of houses being bought and sold. I observed and worked for investors buying and selling houses. I saw the huge sums they were selling these investment properties for—based on my work. My team and I were doing all the hard labor. We were doing the backbreaking, sweaty work for many hours a day. The investors would come by the work sites in suits or shorts and with nice cars, seeming so relaxed and making far more money telling us what to do than we were making by doing the work.

Seeing what was happening, I thought, "I can do that, too!"

I purchased my investment property from a friend of my family. I bought it on a credit line and used credit cards to pay for the materials and complete the flip. That house was a good first flip for me because it had a solid start. While I knew how to do all the construction work, there was definitely a lot more to getting the property marketed and sold, putting money in the bank, and then paying back that initial money I had borrowed to get started. I purchased my first house for $48,000 and ended up putting $37,000 into the rehab. The property resold for $110,000, giving me a $25,000 gross profit on the flip. That was an important win. It didn't make me rich overnight, but I was learning what to do and how to do it.

I used a Realtor to help with that first transaction, and it was a good thing I did. I was initially going to price the house at $6,000 less. That amount almost covered the commissions and fees for all the Realtors—the buyers' agent, my agent, and the seller's agent. I quickly learned that closing costs took a large bite out of my profits on the transaction. The good news was that I was still making a profit. I made about $14,000 on the project after closing costs, and I had only owned the property for 91 days. That is the kind of result that gets you hooked on doing more in real estate. You realize just how much you can make in a short period of time. Even better, you are your own boss. It really wakes you up to what is possible.

With just a handful of house flips a year, you can make more income than most people make at their jobs in an entire year. You may have to run the numbers carefully and put in some real work, but you can make a lot more money without working 14 to 20 hours a day just to barely make ends meet.

From that first flip, I have never looked back. Not every deal has been perfect, but I have constantly learned more about real estate and business, which has kept my real estate business growing. I still own other businesses, but I would never give up real estate.

I can understand how it can be scary to take the leap into real estate investing to just step up your game a bit. Maybe you have to max out some credit cards for a short period of time to make it happen. Maybe you are already burned out and working crazy hours. Maybe your wife and kids want more things and crave more of your time. Unless you commit yourself to giving it a try and just do it, those dynamics in your life won't improve.

You can get started with whatever you have. Your bank account may already be overdrawn, and maybe you can barely scrape out a few hours on nights and weekends to look for house deals and work on them. Still, you can find a way to start, and you'll be hooked after you do that first deal. Then keep learning and doing it better.

Chapter 5

REAL ESTATE INVESTMENT (REI) STRATAGIES

There are many ways to invest and make money in real estate. I'm not sure there is one right or best way to do it. That all comes back to what you have to start with, your strengths, how you enjoy spending your time, and what you are passionate about. Of course, you must clearly define what your personal goals are and what you want real estate to do for you.

I think those who insist there is only one way to do real estate—one superior strategy or best way—aren't being totally transparent and aren't thinking broadly enough. They are either just trying to sell you something or they don't have enough well-rounded experience to offer you. No matter how you get started, there is a spot for you in real estate. You might have to dip your toes into one part of the process just to get going and then find you really love another strategy or other parts of the process. The bottom line is to just get going.

Personally, rehab to retail is my favorite type of real estate deal. I enjoy the process of taking a property that does not look nice or is rundown and outdated, and then improve it to a modern style and quality. I especially love walking through the property after my improvements are completed and seeing that end result. It always brings me a lot of satisfaction and a lot of pride. Then, when you see how that improved property can impact the city and the neighbors and the buyers, doing the flip can be even more rewarding.

I started out by researching and learning the real estate flipping business. The main thing I had going for me was that I had construction industry experience before I started flipping properties. I knew how to do the work. I knew how to find the right people to engage in order to get other parts of the homes rehabbed. I knew that flipping could be done in many different ways on the residential side alone.

When it comes to flipping properties, there are several types of projects. You can wholesale a property. You can "wholetail" property. You can go with a light rehab to sell it as a turnkey rental. You can renovate properties and sell them to a retail buyer.

Wholesaling Real Estate

There are three main ways to wholesale houses:

a. Buy and resell, leaving profit for a house flipper to do the rest of the work.
b. Lock up properties with contracts and flip or assign those contracts.
c. Buy, do some light cleanup or prep work, and resell on the retail market.

It's all about buying low and selling low—like Amazon or Costco.

You really need to be careful and make sure you have the ability to acquire that property if you are going to sign a contract with the seller. You can't just sign up a bunch of assignable contracts and never take possession on any of the properties. You need to have buyers lined up for those properties. You need to have the ability to finance the properties and close, if you have to, and timely assign the deal.

It isn't fair to the seller if you can't acquire the property. You wouldn't like a buyer to contract with you and then walk away on the day of the scheduled closing because they couldn't assign it to another buyer in time. It would waste a lot of your precious time, and you may have missed out on the best buyers, best price, and best profit for your property. Not being able to finish the transaction could cause people who trusted you to lose their homes and life savings.

There is also a lot of confusion out there about wholesaling. Realtors can be very outspoken against it, at least those outspoken Realtors who don't get it and are more focused on fearing the competition than growing their own businesses. Some investors who use other strategies are envious of how easily wholesalers make money. Or they might be tired of inexperienced wholesalers tying up and overpricing many properties and then passing them around through long broker chains and giving bad deals back to the market.

Some states and cities are very stringent on the rules for this type of deal, although wholesaling is not illegal. Wholesaling is perfectly legal and very much appreciated by communities and others when it is done right.

For example, Cleveland, Ohio, is very tough on trying to double close, back to back, on a property. Some lenders won't finance properties that are being flipped. Others love to finance flips.

There are also some basic real estate laws you have to be careful not to break. The big one is that you can't publicly market property you don't own if you don't have a real estate license.

You can sell contracts you own. You can publicly advertise and sell properties you own, even if they are investment properties. If you start doing this for properties owned by others, however, you can get in trouble for practicing real estate without a license.

Generally, when you're wholesaling a property, you'll have an assignable contract with the seller. In some cases, it may be just a standard purchase agreement. At that point, you don't technically own the property, so you can't market it as your own property. You can't ever market the address of the property and show pictures of the property in a mass e-mail or the like until after you close. What you can do before you close is send out e-mails to your own list of existing contacts and offer to show pictures of your pending closings. Provided you have the owner's permission, you can allow people to view the house with a lockbox, or you can take them there.

The other option is to close your purchase of the property and take ownership. Then you are free to market the property as your own.

Not always, but most often, wholesale properties are typically distressed properties that need some work. There also may be owners who are selling a very nice and nearly new property at a discount because they have to move fast. Typically, though, it will be an outdated property with deferred or neglected maintenance. You might even find major repairs, flooding, destroyed roofs, and burned properties. Distressed properties that need the most work are typically resold to investors like me. Rehabbers will then do all the remodeling work before flipping them into rentals or retailing them on the open market.

Depending on the property and current market, "wholetailing" or "prehabbing" may be an option as well.

Prehabbing is creating a clean slate for someone else to do the real renovations and improvements. Sometimes, properties are full of trash, and you just don't know what problems are hidden underneath all that. That can significantly reduce the property value because buyers have to factor in the unknown, and it might just look like a nightmare. If you hire some people to clean out all the trash and maybe even remove much or all of the bad stuff, you create a clean slate. Buyers can better envision a nice end product and thus better evaluate the potential of the property and rehab costs. Just investing $500 to $1,000 to hire some junk-hauling guys for a couple days may give you a nice boost to your profit on the flip.

Wholetailing is when you wholesale to retail by doing the cleanup and some light repairs and then put the property back up for sale on MLS for regular retail buyers. It may not be pretty. It may not be up-to-date. Some first-time homebuyer, however, may buy it to do their own improvements over time. Or a rental property investor might buy it to lease it out.

Wholesaling, however, is the most popular option because you generally don't have to do anything. You don't have to clean, repair, or add improvements. You are getting paid to provide the valuable service of going out to find and negotiate deals at good prices and then serve them up on a platter to other people who want those types of deals. You make an assignment fee if you are just handing over the property. You can add it to the resale price if you are taking ownership. Just make sure you are leaving enough profit for your buyer, depending on what the current market demands. The more clarity you can provide on the condition of the property, the easier it may be to sell it and the more you might get for it.

Turnkey Rental Properties

There is a big demand for rental properties. They are great investments in order to protect wealth and generate strong yields or passive income.

Investors seeking passive income are typically very different than wholesalers and rehabbers. They just want a ready product into which they can put their investment capital. They don't want to spend a lot of time finding deals or remodeling projects. They are willing to pay the price for it. They want something they are able to take out of the box and immediately realize the benefits.

As a flipper, that means you can also be the provider of this product. These investors need a source for these properties and someone to do all the work in order to bring these properties to market.

There are three main things these buyers are looking for:

1. Houses that are rent-ready
2. Income streams
3. An easy process

As a house flipper in this space, you are essentially taking raw inventory and turning it into the product they want.

Remember that whether properties are sold as turnkey or not, they are going to be rentals. Tenants are going to put a lot of wear on these properties. Many things will have to be touched up on the property every time it turns a tenant. If the property is only likely to rent for $1,000 a month in that area, be careful not to over-improve it. If you kill the cash flow, you are killing the property. You should make it nice. You can even make it look like the top end of that neighborhood. Just don't get crazy and have to jack up the price due to spending too much on levels of improvement that won't really be valued by your buyers and maybe even potential tenants.

Refinish the floors or put down carpet. Repaint the kitchen cabinets. Paint the walls. Doing these basics will get the same rent and price as investing 10 times as much. It's all about making the property rent-ready.

What's normally far more important is that you are taking care of mechanical issues and city violations. You want to be sure the home is safe for a family to live in. You don't want to leave structural issues that will prevent a buyer from getting financing or pose big risks to occupants of the property. That might include electrical wiring, furnaces for heating, leaky roofs, and so on.

Where you are selling and renting, along with to whom you are selling and renting, can impact those needs. Landlords who will be renting to Section 8 tenants and those on similar housing vouchers will have to have additional inspections and meet the specific criteria of those programs. Fire alarms, door handles, locks, front steps, and railings can all be specific items that are required for those types of properties.

Cleveland is probably the toughest city in America on its requirements for buyers and sellers through point-of-sale (POS) inspections required by the city. Cleveland wants to ensure that the properties being sold are safe and are being improved. If you are not careful, you can get violations for a lot of little things such as cracked driveways and sidewalks. In some cities, you can receive extreme fines for just letting your grass grow too long.

If you know the housing requirements and market for your area, you'll be able to speed through those checklists and get the house rented or resale-ready. Most of the time, you won't be trying to make the property look like a fabulous celebrity listing. Instead, you are making the property a profitable and working asset.

By doing that, you are stabilizing the investment for your buyers by taking out the guesswork and adding a lot of value. The properties will most likely still be sold at a reasonable discount to boost their appeal because investors are looking for value. So you might market them at 90 percent or less of a fully renovated retail home to really get the attention of the turnkey investors.

Taking this a step further, you can even help place that initial tenant. That lowers the buyers' risk even more and helps them walk into an investment that should be making money and returning them cash flow from day one.

You can market for tenants and lease to them yourself. You can also use a Realtor or property management company to find and place the tenants for you. Just make sure the rent is at a competitive rate and that you have at least a 12-month lease.

To make this turnkey investment even better, you may want to connect the new buyer with a trusted local property management company that will deal with all the tenant interactions, maintenance, accounting, payments, rent collection, and lease renewals. That way, all your buyers have to do is sign the paperwork, close on the property, and then go back to their daily lives and see the money deposited in the bank each month by the property management company.

Rehabbing to Retail

Rehabbing to retail is my preferred real estate investing strategy.

It is not just because the profits can be better or because I actually love doing the remodeling and am passionate about doing that. In my experience, it is a great way to be able to add real value and control your own destiny in any phase of the market. The market is typically in flux, but there will always be distressed sellers and outdated properties ripe to be renovated. There will also always be a demand for housing, especially nice housing, in solid neighborhoods.

This is my favorite space to work because it gives me the highest sense of personal and professional accomplishment. It is also very exciting. I'm continually taking properties that need life put back into them, seeing the finished product, and then watching the new owners' excitement level increase when they see what I have done to the property.

Fixing and retailing properties is not only good for you on many levels, but it is also good for the seller, the neighborhood, the community, the city, and the new residents. You never know how great an impact can be made on a family and the impact that family can go on to have in their community and in the world.

How It's Different

Rehab to retail is different from other flipping strategies, mainly due to how you'll sell those homes to your end buyers. Knowing that in the beginning helps you work backward through the rest of the process of pricing the property and determining what improvements to make.

When you are selling houses retail, you are shooting for the higher end of the market with higher-paying buyers. At least in relation to the other methods we've already covered, you absolutely want full price for the property and are probably publicly marketing that home for sale on MLS.

That means you are competing with a lot of other high-quality homes, and most of those buyers—families and couples, not simple investors—are looking for a home they will live in themselves.

You have to make your home stand out in this retail marketplace. You have to present the property with the level of finishing that resonates and captures the buyers who see it. Those things are your guide to everything else you do.

Smart Retail Rules to Follow

1. Get out of the investment within 30 days.

On this type of deal, you're trying to get a quick exit from the transaction. You've got a lot more invested in the property, and the retail market can change quickly. Every day you hold the property is costing you money, and dollars are coming out of your profit. So, upon completion of the property rehab, you don't want the property to sit on MLS for months and months and months. That is a huge mistake that can bankrupt many new investors on their first retail flip. Ideally, you want to aim to get the flip under contract within two weeks and have a 30- or 45-day closing.

Don't get distracted. To help stay focused and keep things moving swiftly, I recommend finding a niche category and area. Excel in that first. Then you can expand.

2. Have a real remodeling plan.

I would caution you to lay out a real remodeling and transaction plan in advance. Don't just go into a property and start throwing money at it and fixing problems as they arise. You want to have a plan and timeline for the entire transaction, from evaluation through post-closing. You want a scope of work and a tight timeline for scheduling all the remodel work. Know what you are going to do, when you are going to do it, and how much it will cost. Otherwise, you are for sure just buying a money pit.

Even then, there will always be surprises. Everything will cost more than you planned, will take longer to complete than you planned, and will net less than you planned. Count on it. Account for it. Build some room into your cost calculations to be able to navigate those surprises well. I'm proud that during all my years of rehabbing, I have never lost any of my investors' money, though I have had some big surprises and costs that have caused me to absorb some losses myself.

I bought a property back in 2013 and planned to use it as a rental for a few years. Then I turned it into a flip.
It is a classic story of taking a property too far with unexpected costs and hidden repairs.

I purchased the house for $130,000. It was built in 1920 and looked solid from the outside. My plan was to paint and update the kitchen and bath. I started the project, and on the first day of demo, we discovered there was a 2.5" thick metal lath and mortar behind the tile in the bathroom. We next discovered that the kitchen had faulty wiring, and the dining room had some damaged ceiling from the renters who overflowed the upstairs shower. When we removed that damage, we found very unsafe wiring that could burn the house to the ground.

That was a big turning point and a big test. It is in those times that you need to figure out where you stand on moral obligations. Now that I knew what we had, I couldn't close the wall up and sleep knowing that the house had faulty wiring. Therefore, I decided to gut the walls. That doesn't mean it felt good. It was obviously going to get really expensive and add a lot of time to the project.

We continued, dumpster after dumpster, and I saw my money flying away. I realized now that with the house stripped down to bare studs inside and the furnace running fiercely to combat the cold, I had a really huge problem. There was no way I was going to be profitable on this project.

We rewired the house, took advantage of moving some walls to improve the layout, and continued with our improvements. After 4.5 months and $92,000 in renovations, the house was complete. Fresh drywall was finished to perfection. Granite counters were installed in the kitchen along with new stainless-steel appliances. The house was move-in ready.

Since I bought this property as a rental and lived in it for a few months while we were doing renovations on my family's home, I had a special spot in my heart for this property. It really felt like an accomplishment, even though we ended up selling it for just $190,000.

I lost more than $30,000 on the deal, but I did the right thing. I was excited to see that the new owners were a young family who would be able to enjoy many worry-free years in the property. The house sits on a perfect lot to raise kids and abuts a vast area of woods.

Another property we started was going to be a quick two-week renovation. We planned to paint, do the flooring, and then list it. The work didn't go exactly as planned. The previous owner was very handy. He contracted and built the house. He did an awesome job, but when we started taking the switch covers off, we uncovered a major issue. All the lighting was low voltage, which means the house had super small 20-gauge wire running to all the light fixtures. We also could no longer find new switches to replace the existing ones because they were no longer being manufactured for sale and use. We replaced the entire wiring and panel and installed all new LED lights. Of course, that meant more drywall to repair. So from a $130,000 purchase price, we ended up with a three-month renovation instead of the two weeks we had originally planned. The renovation budget exploded to $87,000. Fortunately, we sold the property for $290,000. It still turned out to be a high-profit deal. As my mentor would say, the question is, "How can you find a way to close one of these each week?"

3. Work within Your Circle of Competence.

Working within your circle of confidence is one of Warren Buffet's Golden Rules. It doesn't mean that you don't try new things or get into things that require learning and growth, but it's wise not to get in too far over your head.

That concept has clearly worked out very well for Warren. He probably doesn't know everything there is to know about insurance, Canadian real estate, or such, but he hires the best managers he can and lets them run with it.

When it comes to fixing and retailing houses, there are two big differences in the renovation part of the deal.

1. Structural renovations
2. Cosmetic improvements

A structural item is something that is critical. Most conventional lenders won't finance properties with structural issues. Cities and housing voucher programs will also have a problem with structural issues.

Structural issues include items like these:

- foundations
- electrical wiring and panels
- plumbing
- furnaces
- roofs
- pest infestations
- septic tank leaks

Structural issues are typically bigger, more complicated, and more expensive, and they take longer to remedy. They may even require permits. You will typically need a licensed contractor to handle those things if you don't have your own general contractor license or construction company.

In contrast, cosmetic improvements are more visual than functional updates.

Cosmetic improvements may include things like these:

- flooring
- countertops
- new cabinets
- painting walls
- landscaping
- replacing doors
- lighting and fans
- window coverings

By nature, these are typically easier, faster, and less expensive. In general, it is far more likely that you are able to tackle those things yourself, if needed. For example, if you run out of budget for labor or really can't find a local contractor (I'm not recommending it as a solution or equal alternative to hiring experts), you could head down to your local Home Depot and get some lessons on how to do these things or check out videos on YouTube.

If you don't have a construction background or a general knowledge of construction, I recommend staying out of the process of rehabbing a house or doing any heavy renovating of properties. You can get stuck pretty quickly. Just one or two surprises can add months and tens of thousands of dollars to the projections.

There can be great money for you in real estate, even in homes with sinking foundations, holes in the roof, and in need of gutting. They just aren't the best deals to get your feet wet. I recommend that you start with wholesaling or cosmetic rehabs and then grow into major renovation jobs if you are really drawn to them.

Fortunately, we all have some experience with real estate. I'm pretty sure you've lived in a home. You've probably rented or bought one. That's a great advantage in this industry. Just grow into tackling more and more as you learn.

Narrowing down what type of investment to focus on first will help you focus on what types of properties to look for and how to evaluate and budget your flips. It will help you decide which ones you take on yourself and which ones you pass on to another investor.

Even if you'll never do a DIY and never expect to get into serious structural renovations or additions, the more you know about that part of the business, the better you'll be at whatever you do in the business. You need to know the differences between structural and cosmetic repairs. You need to have a good idea of repair costs and timetables and how your various buyers are going to make money on the property. That will allow you to add value to the flips, price your deals right to make consistent profits, and move your deals quickly.

JVs, Partnerships, and Private Lending

Another way to participate in flipping real estate is through joint ventures, partnerships, and private lending.

Maybe rehabbing isn't your thing, but maybe you have sources of deals, time to find deals, or a lot of contacts interested in buying turnkey properties. Maybe you can bring those abilities to the table and partner with someone who knows the construction side very well. That way, you can split the deals and profits with them.

If you do know the construction and rehabbing side of the business well and have experience, you should be able to find plenty of other investors interested in partnering in their deals. That way, you can gain a bigger interest in the investment than just getting paid as a contractor.

If you have capital or credit lines to invest with but aren't really interested in rolling up your sleeves and getting your hands dirty, then it's worth considering private lending. You can partner with experienced rehabbers with your capital, let them do all the hard work, and get a great passive income return for financing the deal. If that is something you may be interested in, the rest of this book will help you understand more of the process and how to evaluate a good rehabber to partner with.

Chapter 6

MY PROCESS FOR REHABBING AND RETAILING PROPERTIES

Here is my process for successfully flipping a house every time. I have refined and polished my systems to do it after rehabbing and flipping hundreds of houses.

Getting Started

The basic mechanics of flipping a house are not that complex.

1. Find a house
2. Buy the house
3. Make it look prettier
4. Resell it for more than it cost you
5. Get paid
6. Do it again

People buy and sell homes every day—some about a dozen per month. That is not rocket science, and you can get lucky, especially when the market is really booming. Sometimes it can feel almost impossible not to make money. Things can change quickly, however, and the real investors are then separated from the rest when it comes to the details, especially when the market is balanced.

To be able to count on consistently making a profit flipping homes every month, you'll also want to get a handle on the following:

- organizing yourself as a business
- financing your investments and repairs
- choosing your market and niche
- knowing your property values
- calculating your deals and profit
- finding deals
- managing your buy-side and sell-side transactions
- reselling a property quickly
- analyzing repair needs and costs

Get a good foundation to understand the basics, get started, and just keep learning. Learn from experience as well as from partners, mentors, peers in mastermind groups, and the books you read daily.

Getting Organized

Your first step—one you can take immediately—is to register an LLC (limited liability company) in the state where you are doing business. You'll want to make offers in the name of this company, borrow money as this company, put money in this company's business bank account, and do business as this company.

An LLC can help you maximize how much you get to keep by minimizing your taxes, and it will lower your personal liability related to the investment property. Some lenders, investors, and sellers will only want to do business with you if you are legitimately operating as a business.

People will often ask for your operating agreement when arranging real estate transactions and financing them. Setting up your LLC now allows you to take quick action when actually making deals and prevents you from getting stuck on this detail when you are able to locate great opportunities. You don't want to lose out on them because you have been dragging your feet on registering your LLC and creating your operating agreement.

It is in your best interest to hire an attorney to help you with these critical first steps. A business or real estate law firm can help you with these steps. By using an experienced attorney, you'll get custom advice from someone with an interest in helping you succeed since they hope to keep working with you in the long term on other projects you pursue.

Most attorneys have pretty standard templates that they'll tweak for your situation and needs. That shouldn't cost much and is worth every penny. I'd recommend using the best lawyer you can afford.

Since this really isn't that complex and you may not have a lot on the line when you are starting out, you can also DIY this part. Most states will allow you to go online and file your own company in a few minutes for maybe a couple hundred dollars in filing fees. You will then have your tax ID number so you can open a business bank account.

There are now several online legal help websites that specialize in company formation and small business documents. They will cost you a little more than the DIY route but may help you get a better understanding of what you are doing the first time.

Eventually, this will become second nature, and you may end up with a dozen or so LLCs.

QUICK TIP: It is always important to keep some form of mortgage on your properties. I don't like owning properties free and clear. I know a lot of people like to rush to get there, but they can also lose tax advantages and be taking on a lot more liability. If you hold a property, you'll always have some type of payment, even if it is just insurance, property taxes, and utility bills.

In my opinion, free and clear properties can create a lot of vulnerability in asset protection. Properties with liens (loans) are far less likely to become part of a legal dispute due to the mortgage lien. The mortgage holder has first rights to be paid off before any settlement can happen. The mortgage holders have lots of money to pay the best lawyers to avoid any loss, and that works to your benefit. Unfortunately, there are criminals out there who will look for individual owners with properties they own outright and try to find a way to sue them and take them for everything they have. That could be a car accident, a slip and fall on your sidewalk, or something else. Don't be an obvious victim, and the chances of those things happening to you will be far, far less.

Finding the Funding

The biggest excuse you will ever hear for people not getting started in real estate investment or not achieving their potential and goals is money.

There are two things that would be very funny about that if it weren't so sad. First, you'll hear the same need for money at every level of the game, from those starting out with no job, no credit, and being negative in the bank to those with millions of dollars in revenue every year. Second, those with money typically don't use their own once they have it. Don't think like this: "If only I won the lottery and became a millionaire, I could do it." The wealthiest fund managers, billionaires, and investors don't use their own money. They still use other people's money to fund their deals.

Money is an incredibly important tool in real estate. You'll definitely need access to plenty of financial leverage for rehabbing to retail. It just doesn't have to all be yours. There are many sources whether you are just trying to get started or trying to go from 10 house flips a year to 100 or even more.

Hard Money

Hard money has been the common option for wholesalers and flippers for decades. Though many of the lender's terms will change with the market, this type of funding can be ideal for financing quick flips with the least hassle.

True hard money is asset-based lending, which means the loan should be based on the property itself as collateral for the loan and not so much your personal credit and finances as with conventional home mortgage loans. If the value and equity are there, you should get the loan.

It used to be that if there was enough equity in a property and you were buying cheap enough, hard money lenders didn't care about credit, income, assets, or anything else. However, lenders have become a little stricter since the real estate market crash in 2008. They will most likely want to pull the credit of the guarantor and principal behind the LLC and at least look for some assets and experience. They may not have minimum credit score requirements, but they will want to make sure you are not in bankruptcy or foreclosure. They will typically want to see that you have some skin in the game with at least 10 percent to put down and some resources to begin the renovations. They will often finance 50 percent to 90 percent of the purchase price and 100 percent of your repair costs. Money for repairs is generally kept in escrow and used to reimburse you in installments as you complete the various stages of work on the property.

Interest rates and points are going to be higher for hard money than a conventional loan due to lower qualifications. Hard money lenders can also fund deals in as little as a few days or a couple weeks compared to 30 to 60 days with a regular bank. If you are flipping swiftly, the additional costs can be very negligible since you may flip and repay the loan before the first payment is due. Hard money loans are short-term, often only six to 24 months with options to extend as needed. The more experience you have proving you can flip houses, the better terms you can get. When just starting out, that means it may make sense to partner with someone more experienced, pay back a couple of loans, and then do it yourself. Some of those lenders will also partner with you and split the profits on the flip side.

A good next step right now is to reach out to a few hard money lenders who will fund in your area. Try to get preapproved and check their criteria. That way, you can start making offers to buy your investment properties with confidence. You can use websites such as Scotsman Guide and Connected Investors to find lenders who will loan in your state on your type of property and at the loan-to-value (LTV) ratios you are hoping to get.

Private Money

Another avenue for funding your flip deals is private money. That is often the preferred way to finance these types of real estate deals.

Note that many hard money lenders, conduits, and platforms for big banks and Wall Street money call themselves private money lenders. But they are really more like hard money or crowdfunding.

A true private lender is really a private individual or maybe a family office that puts up their own cash to finance real estate investors.

This is something you can't really advertise and market publicly to the general masses—unless you go through the process of creating a fund and doing the SEC (Securities and Exchange Commission) filings and regulatory paperwork. That will cost more money and take more time, but it is something you can work on in the background as you go forward and grow your business.

When starting out, you'll be looking for private individuals and groups with capital to invest. You may find them through friends, family members, or previous coworkers and local contacts. Or you might reach out to private lenders and other cash buyers by looking in public records.

Raising private money is definitely a skill set you can develop. It is not going to be a process that happens quickly or overnight, but it is definitely worth pursuing. You will first have to meet the right people and then build trust by showing them you know what you are doing, but it is very worth it when you get access to this type of money.

Private money is highly desirable for house flippers due to its flexibility. There are some existing and organized private money lenders who already have a clear process and preferred terms. In other cases, you are coaching them and creating custom terms as you go. That can mean lower than market rates, instant funds for deals as you find them, and better terms. They are typically investing in you as a person and your business model, not your credit score, income, or assets. You skip the hassles with banks and their quirks about how many properties you can finance at the same time.

You are also providing these private lenders with great value and a great service. Their alternative is to put their money in a bank or invest in the stock market. That money in the bank is loaned out at higher interest rates, but after all the administrative fees, it returns very little to the investor. How much money do you make on your savings account in the bank? Sometimes it costs you money to keep it in the bank and for the privilege of their borrowing and loaning it out. Crazy, right?

In contrast, private money lenders get to skip all the junk costs and keep all the returns. Even if you are paying them 6 percent or 8 percent, that's a lot more than they are getting elsewhere. They also have the security of investing in solid real estate assets and feeling good about helping people like you instead of making more money for big banks and Wall Street brokers.

There are a couple of ways to structure these private money deals. Most common is when they receive a promissory note from you and have a mortgage lien against the property. They may receive monthly interest payments until you resell the house and they get all their capital back. You can also negotiate more creative options and terms.

Title and property insurance will further protect their investment. If you don't pay them back, they can get the house or negotiate a deal that gives you more time.

Usually, there will still be plenty of equity in the home. For example, they may lend 70 percent of the after repair value (ARV), which gives them a strong position. That's far better than the risk of investing in publicly traded stocks or risky tech start-ups.

Securing this type of funding can take time and a little extra money, but it will be well worth it in the long run. You'll want to retain an attorney to put together the note, mortgage, and deed. You'll want to get out and network to get in front of enough investors who are willing and able to invest in your transactions.

Transactional Funding

Transactional funding can provide 100 percent of the financing with no credit checks, income or asset verification, or appraisals for those focusing on wholesaling, wholetailing, and prehabbing. The catch is that you must have an end buyer already lined up because these loans are usually for only a few days.

Credit Cards, Lines, and Loans

While credit cards are risky, many real estate investors have started out by simply using them to do their first flip or two. You may be able to purchase the property or come up with the down payment and then fund all your repairs by using credit cards, personal loans, lines of credit, and home improvement store cards. Once you make money on those first couple of deals, pay it all back and use your profits to invest going forward. You just have to have a really tight and fast process to know you can resell for a profit.

You may also use home equity lines of credit, credit lines, and bridge loans if you own other real estate.

These strategies can work if you have good credit and are very disciplined about quickly paying back these creditors.

After registering your LLC, you can also begin to build business credit. This offers lots of advantages, even if it takes time to develop. First, it gives you access to more credit than you'd get personally. Second, it separates your personal and business credit. It can come in the form of small business credit cards, lines of credit, and loans. Third, if you ever run into liability issues in your business, it will help keep your personal assets safe. Likewise, if you ever get sued personally or go through a divorce, it may also keep the business assets and income safe.

Mortgage Lenders

Conventional banks and mortgage lenders typically aren't a good source for loans when it comes to house flipping. They move very slowly, are very conservative, and are picky. However, there may be some exceptions such as (1) getting an additional line of credit to finish renovations if you decide to keep a property as a rental and want to refinance on a low-rate, long-term loan or (2) doing a live-in flip and staying for an extended period of time while renovating a home. There are special programs for this such as the 203k loan that can provide funds for the purchase and improvements. Just be careful to read the fine print and be truthful about your intentions. Lying on any application to obtain a home loan, whether from the private or public sector, is a very serious crime. It's just not worth it.

Picking Your Market

Before we get into the transactional details of a house deal, I want to detail the areas we focus on in our projects. When we are rehabbing to sell retail, the property market may differ drastically from other types of real estate investing options.

You need to know your market in order to be able to effectively and accurately assess values, identify a well-priced deal and resale value, and know who your potential buyers are and what finishes they will expect.

You can invest in real estate all over the country and all over the world. Many investors come to Cleveland from other states for the low property prices and high rents. It is far more effective for them to invest as turnkey rental property landlords or private lenders than as house flippers.

It's far easier, less risky, and more profitable when you know the market in which you are investing as a house flipper. To start with, I highly recommend picking an area or two that you can really get to know, inside and out, and then expand your area if you need more volume and diversity.

When you can attract and invest in profitable deals, do really good rehabs, and sell fast for the optimal price, your marketing efforts will go further and your branding will be easier to identify.

Here are some questions you might ask yourself when picking a real estate investment market:

- Which markets and neighborhoods do I know best already?
- Which of those are now ripe for flipping houses?
- In which of those areas can I most comfortably operate?

I tend to flip houses in the Cleveland suburbs. That is the market I know best because I have been living there all my life. I know the players, the market, and the values, and I have learned a lot about these areas on my real estate journey.

Knowing Your Property Values

Knowing your property values is critical. It will help you know how to spot a real deal, how much to offer, how to run your rehab, and how much profit you can realize. Knowing your property values will also increase your credibility with lenders, sellers, buyers, agents, and other real estate investors. If you don't know your property values, you'll be scrambling, working much slower than your competition, and leaving a lot of money on the table.

Property values, selling prices, and buyer activity can fluctuate substantially on both a seasonal basis and over the long term. By growing up in the Cleveland market, I generally know about the various cities that make up the greater metro area. In some, I have very detailed knowledge and even know many of the individual houses. In others, I know more about their approximate values, styles, and cultures.

When it comes to resale and rental values, as well as repair costs, assuming is the worst thing you can do. Always double verify.

I left $10,000 on the table in a transaction because I failed to properly appraise the property. I also wasted three to four months on a property I overpriced and was not getting good traction in the market.

For those reasons, I recommend that you find the market you want to focus on, pick your niche, do your research, and know the end values of the properties. You should be able to instantly see a deal by the price ranges for the properties.

Note: Finding your niche can even reduce your market further. You might find you really have a passion doing homes for veterans or seniors, or working with first-time home buyers and young couples. Your niche could be luxury homes, more rural properties, inner city houses, or starter homes. The more targeted you are, the better your whole system will be. Not being correctly targeted almost put me out of the real estate investment business when I was just starting out. The ongoing effects of how well you target your market will compound over time, whether they are positive or negative.

Early on, I had a small win on one of my first properties. Practically in my sleep, I turned the property around in three months, and I made a little over $12,000 on the deal. Then came a property right after that, and I made another $12,000. That's not terrible, but I know now that it should have been a $30,000 deal. The effect of throwing away $18,000 in profits deal after deal, month after month, is enormous. At just one flip per month, that is almost $216,000 in profits thrown away in the first year. That means nearly $1 million lost in profits in your first four years, and that doesn't count all the gains you lost because you did not have that $1 million to use for investments. Don't be greedy, but don't be foolish and wasteful either.

How do I know that I lost so much on that deal?

A house up the street sold for $210,000, and I sold mine for just $189,000 because I did not know the relative property values in the market. These comparable properties (comps) were similar in every aspect. In fact, some of the features of my property were actually nicer than the higher priced comp.

Market timing can also easily give a property a $20,000 swing in value. I bought my property in June. All my numbers for the flip were based on the current market in June, but I listed the property for sale at the beginning of September.

That is the month when kids are heading back to school and is typically a slow month for real estate sales. We had a fair number of showings, but the buyers looking at that time were not motivated to buy.

The property needed a ton of work and was located in a more rural area. I inflated the value I projected because there were very few comps in the area. *Note: Do not sell yourself on the deal or bend the numbers to work on the very optimistic side because you are only fooling yourself.* I thought I could project the value, no problem. The house showed very well when we were done. The yard and everything in the house looked fresh. However, the timing was bad. The house sat on the market. It didn't sell until spring. That added a lot of holding costs that were coming out of my profit, not to mention the liability risks of holding the property that long. The longer you hold, the higher the risk of tornadoes, freak blizzards, vandals, theft, squatters, and so on.

Once we had a buyer under contract, we got a newer appraisal on the deal. It was a tricky property to appraise because there were not very many comps available. Remember, appraisers are working on behalf of the bank. The bank wants to make sure the collateral asset for the amount loaned is at a value that is safe—in other words, on the low side of potential value. So we lost $20,000 in value on the property, even based on what the buyer was willing to pay, due to the appraisal coming in lower than projected.

Remember this: The value of your investment property is not what the buyer is willing to pay, not unless you are getting all cash buyers all day long. The value of your investment property is going to depend on what the appraiser and the bank's appraisal review team say it is worth.

These are the lessons I have learned on my real estate journey, and I wouldn't take them back for anything.

> *"The only mistake in life is the lesson not learned."*
> *- Albert Einstein*

These lessons made me who I am today. They taught me well, and now I want to pay it forward. I want you to learn from the pitfalls, trials, and tribulations I have already been through so you can jump start your real estate journey. I want you to excel on your journey, too.

When you invest in a real estate deal, it's all about the numbers. Your feelings about the property have absolutely nothing to do with justifying the numbers of the deal you are purchasing. As Warren Buffett says, "Investing is most intelligent when it is most businesslike." Real estate can be emotional. Yes, get excited when you do a great renovation and deliver that home to a great family, or when you help a seller out of a tricky situation, or when you help improve a neighborhood, or when you help another investor make a great return. Just remember to always remain objective about your investment. If you don't, you'll go broke, and all of those potential good things will never be possible.

I've launched properties in the same city, with similar square footage, in similar developments, and with very similar timing. One of the properties sold in just four hours. The other property took two and a half months, and we had put more effort into that property. I thought it was actually a better property, but what I thought or liked about the property did not matter. What matters is what the market considers a good property and what the buyers think is a good price at the time. Lenders and Realtors can also factor into this evaluation process.

How do you know what the value of a property is? How do you know what the market is? It is really smart to stay on top of real estate trends. Ask yourself:

- What neighborhoods are trending?
- What floor plans and architectural styles are coming in and going out?
- What features are closing deals or not closing deals?

Some of your reading time each day should be dedicated to identifying and learning about these things.

It is also important to be able to decipher the valid and reliable data about what is really happening in your unique markets, in the streets, and around the closing tables. Don't just base your decisions on today's headlines. A lot of people use the news to attempt to manipulate the markets and suggest that certain trends are coming. However, the real data and home buyer surveys tell quite a different story. Research and review the real statistics yourself rather than relying on biased or tainted interpretations of them. Talk regularly to local Realtors, mortgage loan officers, and everyday people around town to get a better feel of what is going on in your target market. Again, ask yourself:

- What are the people on the treadmills next to you at the gym saying?
- What are the people at the next tables in the coffee shop saying?
- What are the people at the local farmers' market saying?
- Where are people looking to buy?
- Are people trying to buy expensive micro lofts downtown, or do they yearn for more space and a yard?

There are a number of ways to back up your opinion of values, especially in the early days. You can pull your own comps, although a second opinion could save you time and make you a lot of money, too.

Be forewarned that websites such as Zillow can be very misleading. In some areas, they may be close; in others, they can be way off because their data isn't always up to date or accurate. A 25 percent variation in value is a lot to overpay or undersell for your house in your target market.

Mortgage lenders typically use broker price opinions (BPOs) from local real estate brokers to assess the value of the property securing the loans they have made. Most real estate agents will give you a free comparable market analysis (CMA) with hopes of winning your business and your listing.

There is no true replacement for a full appraisal by a licensed appraiser. It can take time you may not have when comparing many deals, and each appraisal will set you back only a few hundred dollars. Full appraisals can help you avoid much larger mistakes by giving you the most accurate understanding of how a mortgage lender will value the property when financing your end borrower. And that is the most important number for your real estate deal. It is even better when you get an appraisal from a company that does most of the appraisals or appraisal reviews for the highest volume mortgage lender in town.

When going into a deal, you can use a subject-to appraisal, which will tell you the after repair value (ARV) based on the repairs you plan to make. They will say that if you complete this Y scope of work, then the property will be worth X dollars.

Automated valuation models (AVMs) may be a better mid-ground for those looking to fact check their value estimates. AVMs are automated appraisals that are meant to look at the same data as an appraisal but can cost less than $100 and be obtained the same day. Many mortgage lenders use these in place of a full appraisal when doing second mortgages or streamline refinances.

Of course, you must be able to pull your own comps, too. In the long run, with practice, you will be able to accurately value a property in minutes using your own comps. That means looking at the sales prices of recent comparable homes to determine the most likely selling price and fair market value of your investment property.

Factors that appraisers use to compare properties include:

- number of bedrooms
- number of bathrooms
- square feet of living area under air conditioning
- lot size
- age of property
- property condition
- location
- views
- special features such as garages and swimming pools
- community (HOA amenities and dues)

The most accurate comps will be within a mile of your subject property and sold within the last six months. The closer and more recent sales have more weight. In other words, if two identical properties on either side of yours sold for $100,000 last month and your property is identical to them, then yours should also be worth $100,000.

Other types of listing data can be used to support these opinions, but only sold data really counts. You may also look at pending, listed, and expired listings. An expired listing suggests the asking price was too high for the market. Current asking prices really mean nothing but can factor into your opinions. Pending sales can suggest where the market is headed once those sales close and are recorded. Watch these trends closely to determine whether they will take your investment property values up or down.

Again, it is important to also factor in larger cycle changes and seasonal changes. If there are a lot of foreclosures in the works, then values could come down substantially before you get a buyer. Fall can be a slower season, with fewer buyers in the market and less motivation for buyers, but it can also be a good time to buy property from motivated sellers at reduced prices. Winter can make it harder to assess properties for roof condition and do exterior work on roofs, walkways, or driveways. Winter will also crush the effort you put into landscaping.

Late spring and summer are often peak times for buyers who are motivated to make a deal. But late spring and summer can also bring increased competition from other sellers who have been waiting to list their properties. It all depends on your market trends and conditions. It will be quite different, even the opposite, if you are flipping houses in Florida rather than in Ohio.

You can continue to flip houses through any phase of the economy and housing market. You must know when to offer less or when to stretch a little more, when to load up on inventory and when to list.

Assessing and Valuing the Deal

To be a great house flipper, you must know how to walk through a property and what to look for when you do so.

Some investors buy and sell properties sight unseen. Some make great money doing that. But all it takes is one bad deal to undermine everything good you've been doing. It could be a property that doesn't really exist. It could be only a front wall with nothing behind it. It could be a gut remodel instead of needing a couple of cosmetic touches. Any of these bad deals can throw you off your game and eat up all your other profits. It happens. That is why it is always smart to walk through the property yourself before investing. At the very least, have someone you trust walk the property you found and document it for you. If you are not able to do the walk-through or if you are willing to take the risk, then make sure you price your offer in the worst-case scenario. That generally involves a full teardown and rebuild. Remember that it costs a substantial amount of money to demolish and haul away an old house.

When I walk through a potential investment property, I start by walking up the driveway. I carefully look at the condition of the driveway. Is it acceptable? Are there a few blocks that need to be replaced? Is there a whole section of the driveway that needs replacing? Does the entire driveway need to be replaced? The driveway does not need to be in perfect condition, but the condition and appearance of the driveway does make a big impact on the curb appeal of the property.

Cleveland is notoriously tough on regulating the maintenance of driveways and sidewalks, and the city will hit you with a violation if the driveway or sidewalks are cracked and uneven. It doesn't matter if you bought the property with the driveway or sidewalks in that condition. If you are the current owner, the obligation and cost to repair them falls on you.

The next thing I carefully look at is the roof. What does the roof need? Are any of the shingles missing? Are the granules in the roofing material falling off or missing? Are there any apparent areas of leaking? Are there any apparent areas of patching? Are there already five layers of shingles laid one on top of the other? Are there any missing gutters? Is any of the facia trim missing? Is the roof brand new, or is it older but acceptable?

Next I walk through the property on the inside. What's the condition of each room? Does it need a new kitchen, new cabinets, new countertops? What's the flooring like?

Is any trim missing? How do the windows look and function from the inside? Are there missing screens? Do the windows operate properly and easily? Is there any chipping paint? Is there likely lead paint in the house?

Moving on to each bathroom, is the shower surround completely demolished, or is the surround acceptable? Are tiles falling off, or are they secure? Does the bathroom need a new vanity or toilet?

Next, I check the basement carefully to determine if there is any water intrusion. Are there any cracks in the foundation? Does the furnace look acceptable, or is it rusted out at the base? Is the air conditioning new and efficient or old and in need of repair or replacement?

The items I evaluate on this list are all expensive items for your rehab. The more of these items you don't need to replace, the better profit margins this deal will make for you.

There are potential investment properties I have walked away from that I could have acquired almost for free. Even a free property is not a good deal in some situations because it will take more work and money to fix than it will be worth to flip. Rehab costs alone can frequently exceed your purchase price. Sometimes that's okay. It is a matter of how much time and cost is needed to rehab the property and then how soon and how much it can be sold for when you are done.

Go to www.mireiter.com/rehab and get my spreadsheet template to use when you calculate your next rehab property.

Assessing Repairs

There are three ways to assess each element of the potential investment property when you do your walk-through:

1. needs replacement
2. does not need replacement or repair
3. may need repair

If the roof is sagging, if there are fresh leaks inside on the ceiling, and if there are already four layers of shingles, the house will likely need a new roof. That's pretty black and white. You should know the cost for a new roof in your neighborhood. You will need to add that to your repair budget and scope of work.

If it is clearly a brand new roof and the seller is giving you a warranty, that is simple as well.

The tough part is those "maybe" items. For example, the roof is still covered in snow in the winter, but there are brown stains on the ceiling that may not be wet. You don't know if the melting snow is going to reveal a disaster and cause major new leaks or if those are old stains and the roof has been well patched. Most rehab items are not as costly as a new roof, but one or two rehab items of this size for your investment property can make a massive difference in your budget and potential profit margins.

Early on, I used to fix those items in the "it may need it" category, and I did a high-quality fix. I learned that I never got paid back for incurring those expenses.

What I started doing is determining what is going to add the most value to the property and what is in the "may need it" categories. Does it really need windows, or can I simply paint the interiors of the windows? Does it really need a new furnace and AC, or are they running well? Can I have a service technician give the furnace and AC a stamp saying they are operating and functioning fine instead of replacing them? You can spend $250 on a service call versus thousands of dollars to replace a furnace and AC. If it doesn't need it, don't replace it. The same may apply to kitchen cabinets. Can you refinish them instead of replace them? Can you refinish the hardwood under the carpet?

Deciding this will be even more important if you are rehabbing to sell to a landlord or as a turnkey rental. Every extra dollar you spend comes right out of your profit and what they can make in rent. If a tenant is going to destroy the rental home in six months and it will have to be redone for sure with a new tenant in 12 months, then doing a high-end or extensive rehab may not be adding any value to that investment property. You are just pouring your money down the proverbial drain.

You should know that professional home inspectors will look at these main categories when doing their own walk-throughs:

- ROOF: tiles/shingles, flashing, trim, gutters, leaks
- FOUNDATION: trees too close to the house, visible exterior cracks
- YARD: proper drainage, condition of driveway and walkways
- APPLIANCES: function and age
- STRUCTURE: fire damage, water stains, insect infestations
- ELECTRICAL: working outlets and switches, age of electrical panel
- PLUMBING: noisy pipes, leaks, water pressure
- GENERAL: condition, updates needed
- SPECIAL FEATURES: garage, pool pumps, and more

You can also visit the International Association of Certified Home Inspectors' website (https://www.nachi.org/) for a copy of their home inspection checklist.

The American Society of Home Inspectors (ASHI) lists what their inspectors found to be the most frequently found issues:

- FAULTY WIRING: wires without wire nuts, open junction boxes
- FAULTY PLUMBING: low water pressure, water stains on ceilings
- POOR DRAINAGE: soggy areas in the yard, basement leaks
- BAD GUTTERS: clogged gutters, basement leaks
- FOUNDATION FLAWS: small cracks, sticking doors and windows, basement leaks
- POOR MAINTENANCE: chipped paint, worn shingles, cracked driveway

ASHI says these issues are not deal breakers and are actually relatively easy to fix with the right contractor. You do need to assign a cost to repair them, however.

Again, make sure you add to your list any items that you know will be issues with the local building department and city zoning code, as well as Section 8 or Eden programs if it will be a rental.

Making the House Sexy

One thing I do not discount or budget on-the-cheap is what I call "making the house sexy."

I know this may be confusing because I have mentioned some areas not to overspend on. It is true that over-improving can be one of the most common (and one of the worst) mistakes that brand new house flippers make. Failing to spend a little more on the right areas of your rehab, however, can cost you a lot more in the resale value of your investment property. I'll go into detail about where to spend more in your rehab budget and why spending more on the right areas is necessary.

Have you ever walked through a production builder's model home? They have awesome lighting, $100,000 worth of furniture placed in and throughout the house with beautifully installed and manicured landscaping outside and around the house.

All these details are designed to do just one thing when a potential buyer is walking through the house—drive emotions and feelings about the property.

It may not add a dollar to your appraised value, but getting buyer attention, getting them into the home, and wowing them with the appeal of your property is 90 percent of the battle. You are an objective business person acting in the real estate market. Retail consumers are emotional creatures who act on impulse when they buy. That is why footwear companies offer $5,000 sneakers for sale. Bernard Arnault, CEO of LVMH Moët Hennessy (Louis Vuitton and Moët & Chandon) recently displaced Bill Gates as the world's second-richest person with a net worth of more than $100 billion. He said, "We want our buyers to make sound financial decisions, but emotions sell, and the math inevitably comes second for them." So start thinking how to drive emotions and feelings about your property when doing your retail flips. Ask yourself these questions:

- Can I add a $300 chandelier in my flip's dining room that matches the style in a house that's a few hundred thousand more than this property?

- Can I add trending hard-surface countertops to my flip that gives it the WOW factor?

- In the hall bathroom of my flip, can I install a shower surround and tile?

Then ask yourself this: What's my number for the one WOW piece in every major room of my flip? What's my number for the over-the-top dining room chandelier? The trending kitchen countertops and modern-looking cabinets? The bathroom tile surround? The bathtub? The better quality vanity? You'll know these WOW numbers in your head after a couple of deals.

Add these WOW numbers to your up-front math and rehab budget. Do not back these important details out of your budget in order to make the project work. If these expenses are not feasible when you do your up-front math, then the house is not a good investment property. You can't count on that flip being quick and profitable if you can't make the house sexy.

My team bought a property that the owner had purchased at a sheriff's sale. He and his family had moved in, but then they had gotten into a domestic dispute. As a result, they sold the property to a real estate wholesaler from whom I buy a lot of investment properties. After we took possession of the property, the neighbors said they were happy to see us purchase the property because we started taking care of it and did not disrupt the neighborhood. The old owner had played loud music late into the night, and the police would show up to silence the noise that was creating a nuisance for the neighborhood.

We showed up and filled two dumpsters with junk from the property. We immediately budgeted our WOW numbers and started renovating. We installed a new kitchen. We gutted and installed a new bathroom. We replaced the windows. We installed a new AC unit. We installed new flooring. We removed large overgrown plants from around the outside of the house. We beautifully landscaped the yard around the house. We prepared and painted the inside of the house.

We purchased that property for $100,000 and then put $43,000 into the rehab. We sold it for $187,000. We made a reasonable profit, but I actually first listed the property without staging it. After we staged it, I uploaded pictures of the staged property for MLS. The walk-through feedback from Realtors and buyers changed drastically. That was the first property we ever staged.

There is something about people being able to visualize what the space can be turned into that makes a huge emotional appeal. We ended up selling the property to a husband and wife. Their kids were grown, and they had been looking in the area for more than a year. The property flip was a perfect fit for them. It was also a perfect fit for the neighborhood. I periodically still text and speak with the new owners. It is very satisfying to be able to have great relationships with people who work with you. That is one of the things I enjoy most about investing in real estate.

The profit is great, but more than that, you helped the wholesaler who helped the stressed-out family make some money and move on with their lives. You helped the neighbors with a more peaceful community. You helped the new owners who will enjoy every day in the house you flipped. You gave them a nice place that their children and grandchildren can visit and create special family memories. That's really big. That's priceless.

There are many ways you can stage a home to sell, even if you are starting out on a tight budget. There are some home staging services that sometimes collect their money after closing. That can be a big risk, but because it is a necessary WOW expense, you must consider it.

There are also home or furniture stores that may offer years of zero interest payments or even no payments for a while. You can use those options to purchase your own inventory of staging furniture and accessories and then move the staging inventory from house to house. That will save you the staging expense of a staging company. You can also offer the staging inventory as a package deal with the flip if the buyer wants to include it for the right price and terms.

There are even rental stores for kitchen appliances, entertainment electronics, giant TVs, and full room suites. You can just return them when you sell the flip. The rental stores will usually deliver and pick up their rental inventory at the flip.

Then there is the trending option of virtual home staging. It will not have the same emotional impact as an in-person walk-through, but for a couple hundred bucks, you can have photos of your flip virtually staged. There are even apps that will allow buyers to see their belongings or their colors in the flip. One of those apps is Curate, created by Sotheby's International Realty. You can get Curate on your Apple or Android phone and share it with your buyers.

Picking the Right Buyer

Right now you might be saying, "Well, I know I can cheap out on all these things, and I can still flip the house in my market for a reasonable profit."

You might be right. You certainly can put cheap finishes in your flip, but it will likely take longer to sell it. I am looking to close a flip in a week or less. I want my property to appear nicer than all the other comparable properties on the market so it will sell quickly.

When you are looking at comps, you must check out what those competing houses look like and how long they have been listed. You also must determine the average days on the market for properties in your own market.

I want to create a bidding war on my property. I want to be able to pick the buyer and contract the deal that I like most.

We've all heard the saying about not putting all your eggs in one basket. When you have a property sitting on the market for six months and one offer finally comes through, you will take that offer. It doesn't matter what the offer is, you are taking it.

Then, as you move through this offer to closing and see the profit margin on the flip, which is less than you wanted and what you thought the house was worth, you'll start cringing at the other terms. You might have to settle for a closing date 60 days out. Then you realize the contract has a contingency that relies on the buyers selling their current house first, and you're paying a bunch of the buyer's closing costs. Then you get into the inspection phase, and they ask you for more concessions on the property. Holding a flip too long makes me very nervous. There is so much that can go wrong, and you can easily end up taking a loss. The chances are that you will end up losing more and more because you have to flip to cut your losses.

I like to take the strongest offer and get it signed quickly. I also like to have a person in the back-up offer position. I like to close in 30 days and keep up the momentum through the process.

Can you see how this fast tracking does not work when you are just trying to match the standard of all the other houses on the market in your price range?

Your house should be the one for all the real and qualified buyers in that price range right now. You want to give value while still maintaining your profit. If you get this right, buyers will fight over your home. Then you get to dictate the terms, and anything extra you invested in these star features will more than pay for themselves when you reduce your closing time and reduce your risk.

Let's look now at some key provisions and clauses you ideally want in your contracts.

As-Is

It is much easier to sell a property as-is—in its current condition and just as it is. A contract that is not an as-is contract will typically make the deal contingent on the inspector not finding any repairs, or it will have a dollar amount (or percentage of the sales price) that any found repairs should not exceed—for example, 2 percent of the purchase price.

Inspection Contingency

The buyer should always have the right to inspect the property, even in an as-is deal. You do not want to give the buyer any more than 10 days to get this done, and preferably less. In a really hot market, sellers will make buyers do inspections before going to contract and will require buyers to waive their right to inspections or renegotiations for repairs after the purchase agreement is signed.

Financing Contingency

With the purchase offer, the buyer should provide you with either proof of funds to pay all cash or a preapproval letter from a reputable bank or mortgage lender. Many Realtors and sellers will demand it even before showing the property. If the buyer needs financing, the contract can be much less certain and take longer to close than with a cash transaction. There are many things that can go wrong in the process. Buyers may not qualify for their loan, the appraisal can come up short, buyers may lose their jobs while waiting to close, or the bank may just run out of money to lend. Any financing contingencies in the contract should also have a very short period to be resolved.

Appraisal Contingency

You can't really force a buyer to buy your property if they need financing and the property doesn't appraise. They just may not have the extra money to put down. If that happens, you can renegotiate or cancel the deal. By removing an appraisal contingency, the buyer's earnest money deposit can become nonrefundable.

Even though appraisals can be really quirky, you should be pretty confident that your property will pass before you get to that stage. Then it is really a moral question of whether you really want to take the unfortunate buyer's deposit money when the deal fails due to no fault of their own. While you may choose not to take their deposit, any Realtors and their brokers involved in the failed deal may also go after that deposit money for their commissions and fees.

Kick-Out Clauses and Backup Offers

It's always wise to have backup offers. Although you want to be really confident in the buyer and the offer you accept, having plan B is just smart. Keep marketing and accepting backup buyers so you won't have to start from scratch if the original deal falls through. That puts you in the position of taking offers when you are in the strongest negotiating position rather than when you are desperate and the market may have changed.

Extensions on Closing Dates

Delays happen, especially if you are retailing your houses and counting on buyers who need financing. You may need to agree to an extension of your closing date. Often this comes up at the last minute when the buyer's lender creates a new underwriting condition. While not ideal by any means, granting an extension may still be less risky and less costly than finding a new buyer or even digging into the process with your backup offer. The deal may still not work out, even with the extension, but do the math. You can reduce your risk even further in these cases by asking for an additional deposit to be put in escrow or making the escrow deposit nonrefundable.

Pricing Your Deals for Sale

How do you establish the list price for your investment property when you are ready to sell?

You should already have your comps or some form of market valuation. You also need to know you can afford to sell at the comp or market price or if you can undercut the competition with a slightly lower than comp or market price to create a faster sale and a bidding war that may actually have you selling for even more.

Begin by adding up all the figures for your large-ticket expenses. That will take significantly longer on your first property. Get help where you can to reduce risk of error, and be sure you aren't overlooking anything. In addition to an inspection and quotes from multiple contractors, you can also get help evaluating your costs from your mortgage lender and title company. Your real estate attorney or closing agent can help prepare a net sheet that will show your estimated net proceeds based on a given sales price or deal scenario.

Once you've done this a few times, you'll be able to conjure up the numbers in your head in a few minutes.

Be sure to add a cushion for contingencies. Add at least 10 percent to 20 percent on top of your overall rehab figure. The more cushion, the better. The less experienced you are and the less risk you can tolerate, the more you want to pad these numbers.

Take those numbers and add them to the asking price of the property. Include any financing and closing costs on the buy side and sell side. You should be able to eventually break this down to a rough percentage in order to do quick calculations on the go. There are free closing calculators online that will give you the average percentage in your area. That percentage will generally be higher on lower-priced properties due to fixed costs but lower on high-priced properties. There may be exceptions in states such as New York where there are additional "mansion taxes" for more expensive homes. Don't forget to factor in any Realtor fees.

Know what the after repair value (ARV) of the property will be.

I also normally calculate an asking price (the price I will list and would like to get), as well as a take price (the price I will accept).

Now add all of your costs together. Subtract that from your resale price. That is your anticipated gross profit.

Don't forget to account for your own income taxes and capital gains taxes generated by the flip.

Tax obligations are typically omitted from consideration in those "reality" TV shows. The last thing you want is to be surprised with a bill from the IRS for tens of thousands of dollars when you haven't set aside the money to cover that tax bill. With a good accountant and the right structures, you can pay a lot less tax and make a lot more money investing in real estate than working at a regular job.

The other item not to forget is any partnerships or special arrangements with those who are funding your deals. Be sure to calculate your profit splits. Make sure the deal still has a good return for you after your profit splits are paid.

One cost that can make or break you is holding costs.

Holding costs include the following:

- interest on financing
- insurances
- property taxes
- utilities
- temporary home staging items
- association dues

On low-end properties, that might not amount to much cost. For high-end deals, that can be thousands of dollars coming out of your profit each month. Break your holding costs down to a daily rate. Know the difference in your profit if you sell in a week, a month, or six months. Every day you are holding the investment property, there is risk. On a side note, if you are using Realtors to list your properties and they know your houses are going to attract offers in the first week (and maybe even the first day they go online), their job gets a whole lot easier and more efficient than a six-month or longer listing. You can use that to negotiate lower commissions with your Realtor.

Put simply:

- Take the most likely resale price based on ARV.
- Subtract all your acquisition, rehab, and other transactional costs.
- That establishes the potential gross profit margin.

- Decide if that margin is enough to be worth doing the flip.

Calculating Your Profit

The other way to evaluate and price deals and then calculate your profit is to determine how much you need or want to make and use it as your lens to evaluate all deals. Know your maximum offer for the property and decide your lowest acceptable price on the resale side. How much you need to do the flip and what it's worth when completed are all up to you.

That may be influenced by how much you were making at your last job, what your real estate investment strategy is, and whether any partners or lenders are involved.

You can set a flat minimum fee you want to make. For example, as a wholesaler, you might set an assignment fee of $2,500, $5,000, or $10,000. If you are set on returns, it may be 8 percent, 14 percent, 25 percent, or more. If it is a property that is going to have an ARV of $150,000 or less, I would not be doing a deal that would have less than $25,000 to $30,000 of profit.

If you are running a deal and your initial figures come in at only $10,000, double check your math or move on. It's not a deal. That $10,000 might sound nice, especially if you plan on doing 100 deals a year. But unfortunately, once you're finished with the project, there are going to be some costs that put a hole in your original projections. Maybe you missed something in the rehab budget. Maybe the property sat on the market longer than you anticipated. Maybe a change in season or comps takes $10,000 off the resale value. That $10,000 is not enough insulation or upside potential to take that gamble. If you can get out of it for a couple thousand in the red, multiply that by three or six properties you will do over your first season. That's a recipe for disaster. Plus, it's just not fun.

My math changes for this figure with a higher-valued property. If you are looking at a house with an ARV of $300,000, there may be more potential profit, but there is also more risk. A 10 percent fluctuation in values can wipe out $30,000 in profit. Your funding will cost you more, and your holding costs will be higher. Therefore, a minimum profit potential of $30,000 to $60,000 is required to make the flip worth doing.

The more you can control or eliminate the deal risks, the less you might have to pad your numbers to account for those risks.

If the wholesaler, Realtor, or person from whom you are purchasing a property is your brother, your sister, your best friend, or someone you've had a relationship with for 20 years, you must still calculate the ARV for yourself. Check comps for yourself. If you are doing turnkey, check the rental comps yourself, too. Double-check the property condition yourself. Make sure you cover as many items as possible. Get additional contractor quotes for yourself. Don't trust rough estimates from the seller. Get a professional home inspection. It may cost you $300, but it is so worth it. If you're serious about the deal, $300 is a much better investment than losing thousands of dollars and months of time on a project.

Check the title records for the property. Make sure the seller is the legitimate owner and that there aren't any other owners who will need to sign the sales contract. Look carefully for any liens. If you are willing to take the risk of not getting title insurance and you don't have a lender who will make it mandatory, at a bare minimum you should be paying for a professional lien search and chain of title before making an offer. Then update that search just before the closing to discover any changes that will impact the deal.

Having multiple exit strategies will further reduce your investing risks and give you much more peace of mind when getting into deals. Your A game may be rehab to retail. That doesn't mean you should never use other exit options. You should know the value of the deal for all your main exits. The more that are viable, the better. If you have a viable plan B and plan C, that deal is a lot safer, and you won't lose sleep over it.

For example, you may want to fix and flip retail at the best possible exit price. If you can't get those premium finishes done or the retail buyer market seizes up, can you sell it to a turnkey investor for a little less by putting a little less into the flip. Can you turn the flip into a rental for yourself and sit on it for a year while still covering the mortgage payment and a couple hundred in cash flow each month from your rental income? Would you live in it temporarily if you had to wait the season out? If you dig in and find the rehab a lot harder than you thought, are you buying it cheap enough that you can just wholesale it to another rehabber with more experience or who has better deals on materials and labor?

You can also get an edge by knowing what the ARV will be in the hot spring or mid-summer market or where the ARV may land if you are finishing your project in the fall.

Negotiating with the Seller

Sellers have a way of painting a very bright and flowery picture of their properties. Realtors are professionals at this.

Some wholesalers use phrases such as "a quick in and out" or "knock off the ugly." We all know "handyman special" can be code for complete disaster, just like "cozy" means ridiculously small.

As retailers, we have to deliver better work. Nice finishes matter to the homebuyers who are purchasing our homes. We aren't going to cover up mold or stuff newspaper in gaping holes and paint over it.

Consumers will know when they walk into a property if it has gone through a DIY for a slash-and-dash flip or if it has been professionally renovated. In fact, homebuyer surveys show that obviously DIY homes can be a huge turnoff. Buyers don't like amateur work and can be scared away by what may be lurking underneath. If it is clearly sloppy on the surface and the details aren't right, there is probably something worse underneath. Buyers may not understand the cost difference, but they can spot quality and care in your work.

Rental-ready finish levels can work in a lot of markets, and wholesalers typically work with investors who want to do the flip as cheaply as possible.

Many wholesalers do not understand the retail flip market, but even if they do understand it very well, they are trying to maximize their profits. I don't fault anybody for maximizing profits, even though we are trying to create win-win-win deals for the sellers, the flippers, and the buyers.

I am okay with wholesalers making markups and good profits if they are providing a valuable service by bringing me a deal that has value with numbers that work. I'm okay as long as I can purchase the property at a price that's acceptable to me. It really doesn't matter how much the wholesaler makes.

There is something you will discover about those who are truly wealthy. They aren't penny pinchers, and they aren't wasteful, but they make decisions based on value.

At the end of the day, the wholesaler needs to know that you can complete the transaction because you have the funds available and you're going to complete the transaction on time. Once the wholesaler sees that you can complete your deals on time, you will gain credibility and trust. They will recognize you as a serious buyer, and future negotiations with them will be easier.

I prefer to know what purchase price the wholesaler has paid for a property I am evaluating, so I will ask them. Some newer wholesalers (or more greedy ones) don't want to tell you because they think they will lose the sale or not make as much profit on it. The truth is that wholesalers always buy their real estate inventory at a great price, and if I can negotiate a purchase price that gives them a reasonable profit but still allows me to generate a great value, I have no problem making that deal.

When the house closes, I will know exactly how much the wholesaler paid for the property. I can also easily check the website of the county where the property is located to research the real estate and financial records for that property. It's nice to know when wholesalers are trying to give you value with a fair purchase price. If the wholesalers, without doing any of the rehab work or taking any real risk, will make more than you by trying to sell you a very tight deal, that says something about them. Others are happy making a modest profit and like to help others make money. Which type of wholesaler you are dealing with will make a difference in how much work you will have to do when screening each deal. If you find and work with a really good wholesaler, you will know that when they call you, they will have a real deal, and you will take it. That quick turnaround, based on mutual trust and credibility, is better for everyone.

Many of the same factors apply when dealing with Realtors and private homeowners.

Most Realtors, when dealing with strangers for the first time, have little expectations of ongoing business. Most of their leads don't turn out. They are flooded by newbie investors every day who don't end up buying anything. If you can prove yourself to the Realtor by demonstrating your ability to do real estate volume, they will also treat you with credibility and trust. Instead of trying to squeeze more money out of you on one deal, they will look at the bigger picture with the greater value of doing multiple and very easy-to-close deals with you every month. They can make a lot more money consistently by charging you less. Make them look good in negotiations by giving them enough financing and information to present your offers well, and they will work hard not to lose your business.

Sometimes just explaining your process and describing what you plan to do will show the seller or Realtor that you know how the numbers really work, and that is all they need to have confidence that you will complete the transaction and accept your offer to purchase their property. They want a win, but they may not be realistic in the beginning. You can help them understand that they aren't going to get a better deal by waiting and that negotiating a deal makes sense for both of you.

When dealing through a real estate agent or directly with a private homeowner, the more confidence they have in you as a buyer, the better the negotiations will go. The most feared risk in a real estate transaction is that the buyer will not be able to close, and it should be that way. Neither you nor the wholesaler can afford to be tied up for months in a contract that doesn't close. There are too many inexperienced investors and dreamers who are not able to close the deals they offer to make. Many just want to option properties in hopes of wholesaling them, and then they can't find a buyer or timely close.

Show the sellers and Realtors how strong a buyer you are. Show them you have the funds or the financing required to put down a deposit with few contingencies. Some will care that you are going to do a good job on the home, which will benefit the neighborhood and a new family. Others may care more about the numbers and their needs in the deal. Show them how you have the best solution for a deal, whether that is price, speed of closing, or something else.

Some sellers and Realtors may be convinced that you have the best solution for a deal when you break down for them just how much work, investment, and risk you'll have to take on as the buyer. Often, they just haven't thought about it from your perspective. They haven't considered that you will be investing another $30,000 to rehab this property, that every day you hold the property will cost you money, that you may be absorbing losses in a declining real estate market, and so on.

It may mean something to the sellers and Realtors that you have experience and a positive track record flipping real estate. It may mean something to them that you will take care to make this home really healthy and beautiful for a new family in need at a reasonable price, thus preserving the neighborhood. Others will just be stuck on a figure and will refuse to even think about the math. They won't bother to take the time to think about or consider the deal from your angle. Walk away and encourage them to come back when they are really ready to sell, even though your offer will probably be even lower by then.

The more you learn about the seller and any agents involved, the better equipped you will be in your negotiations. They can come from a variety of situations and have a variety of priorities.

When your incentive for making a deal is that you can close this week, that incentive will not motivate the seller to make a deal if they can't move out of the property for a month. Some sellers will be stuck on the cover price, no matter how little sense that makes. In many cases, they may be facing a tight deadline they need to meet, they may have a lien they need to satisfy, or they may be desperate to distance themselves from a trouble tenant. The same is true for Realtors. Maybe they need a quick close to earn a bonus and override on commissions this quarter. Maybe they pride themselves on sales prices, regardless of all the concessions in those contracts.

Asking and then truly listening along with doing your property research and other due diligence will make you better prepared to negotiate. Know where you can give and take and where you won't give and take, but remember that everyone likes to feel they won something in their negotiations.

Steps to Acquiring the Property

In today's market, there are many ways to acquire properties.

Here are some of those options:
- Outbound marketing to motivated sellers
- Using real estate agents and MLS
- HUD homes
- Public real estate auctions
- Bank-owned properties
- Referrals from attorneys and finance professionals
- Acquiring deals from real estate wholesalers

Some of these may work better than others for you and your talents. They may depend on the resources in your target area and the state of the economy at the time you are buying.

If you have all cash, you can bid for properties at auctions or find properties online. Those options can be very competitive, and you really need to know what you are buying before you close. The U.S. Department of Housing and Urban Development (HUD) auctions off foreclosed properties. There are good deals to find, but some options depend on where and when you are looking.

You can—and should—build a referral network for real estate deals. Just like raising capital from private investors, that can take time, so don't expect to instantly build a network of referrals. Just make it an organic part of your week. Get out and network, do lunches and dinners and more. Find some contacts and ways to work together with bankruptcy, divorce, and probate attorneys, as well as mortgage loan officers, bankers, and financial planners.

You can sometimes pick properties right off the public MLS system, although those deals are often overpriced and very competitive. Realtors can help you find off-market deals and pocket listings that may not be publicly available online. Getting your own real estate license is another option that may give you some additional access. Keep in mind that getting your own real estate license will be time-consuming and costly and will add additional risk. As discussed earlier in this book, there are some things you cannot legally do when you have a real estate license that you can legally do without one. Real estate agents can find you deals, so don't write agents off like many investors do. Realtors will often reduce their commissions on your purchases if you are using the same agent to relist the properties after your rehab. Sometimes they can receive a commission in four ways (buyer side and seller side on your acquisition and exit, and maybe leasing, if needed, in between). You should be sure to negotiate a fair commission deal with any real estate agent.

Maybe you are already a marketing genius and love using door-to-door selling, direct mail, radio shows, billboards, podcasts, Google ads, and social media marketing such as Facebook. That is the way many, many investors try to do business these days. If marketing isn't something you've already mastered and you don't have a great marketing budget, then be careful. There is a lot of marketing services hype out there. You can go broke on marketing services really fast. Those options can help you keep a consistent long-term flow of deals in your pipeline. Just be wary of betting the precious money in your buy and rehab budget on things you don't really understand.

You can purchase properties directly from sellers, buy distressed properties from wholesalers, or acquire bank-owned properties. You can purchase properties at tax lien auctions or sheriffs' sales. You can approach probate attorneys to find properties or research properties on MLS. When you find a property with numbers that give you the right value, then you make an offer.

Remember that time is your most precious asset, but never forget the ultimate goals of your ideal business model. On top of the cost of finding good deals (real estate investors often end up spending hundreds of dollars just for a lead), the time you spend searching for leads on the acquisition side is really costing you. If your goal is just to make $1 million a year in real estate and you are willing to work 40 hours a week during all 52 weeks of the year, you still need to make $481 per hour. If you aren't coming up with a potential deal each day and are putting in eight hours of searching for deals each day, you probably aren't going to hit that goal.

You can mail out terrible marketing material or put up an ugly Craigslist ad and get 100 calls in a week. If none of those are real deals, however, you'll be down more than $19,000 in a week of lost time, putting you further away from your goal. Most people don't make close to $500 an hour cold calling or doing Internet marketing. If you want to use those options, outsource them to someone you can pay at a lower hourly rate than your time is worth while you focus on closing deals.

There is really so much to do as a rehabber, especially when you first get into the business. Aside from all the corporate, business, and accounting tasks, you have to find the deals, screen the deals, fund the deals, fix them up, and stage to flip them. Each one of those areas is a big role to be mastered. The more you can focus on the one area you do best, the better. You can engage in the others later, if you like, but if you spread yourself too thin by trying to do it all, the chances are you will not get very far very fast.

If you are an ace at finding deals, that's great. Contract out the rehab and use a Realtor to sell the deal. If you are great at staging and selling properties, focus your time on that part of the flip. If you love the renovation part, dig into that portion of the flip and bring in help on the other parts.

Personally, I like to purchase my deals through wholesalers because the rehab to retail flip is really my passion and preference. The wholesale properties can add a lot of value if you find good ones and know how to work well with the wholesalers. I have wholesalers who know the type of properties I like to buy. They know my criteria for what is a deal for me and what is not. They may find other deals and sell them to other investors, but I will often get first crack at the ones that fit my criteria. That is because the wholesalers know I am a serious buyer and would rather knock out a fast and fair deal with me than try to shop their properties around.

My wholesalers really know the business and look for buyers who can quickly close on transactions.

These wholesalers are generally making $5,000 to $10,000 per transaction when I am purchasing from them. They have spent thousands of dollars on marketing each month. They have met with at least 10 or 15 homeowners. They have convinced those owners to sell at a great price and under contract. They have done some type of due diligence and screening to make sure the numbers I need will work on the property. Then they bring those properties to me on a silver platter so I can choose. All that heavy lifting has already been done by the wholesaler, and that's worth something. It is a valuable service because I don't have to search out the properties and can focus on what I'm really good at on that property flip.

Using wholesalers allows me to be a little pickier with the properties that I do purchase because I have spent nothing to find the properties. I don't have to throw $5,000 or $10,000 at marketing for the month and just hope I get lucky with a good deal lead that will pay off that marketing expense. I don't have to make a risky gamble on a crazy deal just to get my marketing money back. I don't have to look at hundreds of deals and run the numbers on all of them and speak to all those people just to sift through everything and find one or two viable deals. I don't have to spend my money on gas or hours of my time in those houses having conversations that may not go anywhere.

Using wholesalers enables me to at least break even on my deals more easily than spending money on my own marketing just to find the leads for a deal. In fact, I do far better than that. The wholesalers are taking all the risk, and I get to cherry pick the very best deals with the best profit margins. They can sell the properties I don't want to someone else.

Plus, I get to spend my time focusing on the rehab where I can really add value and enjoy what I'm doing. Imagine if I spent 40 hours a month finding deals. What time would I have left to do a good job rehabbing and retailing them? I would have done all that work acquiring the flip, which I don't enjoy, and then would be burned out when it came time to do the rehab, which I do enjoy. That's if I hadn't blown my rehab budget on my marketing time and expense.

The choice to source wholesale deals is also about consistency and volume. If you try to do everything yourself, you're only going to get so far. Your income and financial survival will always depend on your personally nailing this month's hot marketing trend and being up to sell to those people. You can't just get lost in searching for deals, then rehab one, sell it, and start the cycle over again unless you are only going to do it as a part-time hobby. If you want consistent income every month that you can count on to pay your bills, and if you want to hit bigger income goals, then you need to get a constant flow of deals on your desk or phone every day.

This is about being focused on the business process. Like it or not, rehabbing is a business. If you ignore that and treat it as a hobby, you'll only get paid like it's a hobby.

Going aimlessly through your days in many directions with no systems to organize your efforts is a recipe for being broke, stressed out, and really unhappy. There is no need for that.

As you go along, you want to regularly take time to take a step back and put on your business owner hat. Take a look at where you can create systems to make your business model more effective, and then determine where you can find other people to do the busywork less expensively than you and ensure your model is operating like a business that can grow and deliver to achieve your goals. It's like a maze. You can run into a maze and hope you find your way through it with a lot of trial and error. Chances are you'll get lost quite a few times, even if you do make it out on the other side. Or you can use one of those little drones to go up and see the broad picture of the maze to find your way directly through it in just a few seconds and avoid getting caught in all the weeds.

Whether this is your first deal or your 10th deal, you will probably still be searching for and refining your niche area of the home styles and the cities where you like to work, along with the best practices to rehab those properties and determine how far you want to take them. That's okay. Those are all questions to regularly ask yourself and how to continually improve your business model. The more often you look at the big picture and make adjustments, the sooner or more likely you are to achieve your end goals.

Finding Good Wholesalers

If you do choose to go the wholesaler route and buy assets that way, make sure to find a few good ones. You never want your entire business to rely on just one other person or company. That's a big risk. Having three to five good ones working for you will give you more options and consistency. Nonetheless, the more business you give individual wholesalers and wholesale businesses, the more clout you will have with them, the better they will take care of you, and the more efficiently you can flip your properties.

Watch out for bogus wholesalers and those who do not know what they are doing. Unfortunately, there are a lot of them out there. Everyone has to start somewhere, but there are those who give wholesalers and real estate investors, in general, a bad name by being too greedy or just not knowing what they are doing.

You'll easily spot many bogus wholesalers because their numbers are so far off. They either don't know what a deal is or they are just trying to pull the wool over some new rehabber's eyes.

Then there are other bogus wholesalers who get involved in all kinds of crazy broker chains. Three or four other "wholesalers" get involved, all with their fingers in the pie, and there may be only one holding a real contract with the seller. Avoid those messy situations.

Network at your local Real Estate Investment Association (REIA) and ask others in the business for referrals. People will pretty quickly either get a good name for themselves or a bad one, depending on how they do business.

Try a deal, complete your own due diligence, and test the referral sources before loading them into your pipeline.

Closing on the Buy Side

You have found a property that you love, and you want to invest in it. How do you get from finding it to owning it and getting your project started? The property looks like a good match on paper, and you've put your boots on the ground to personally see it. You have run through your inspection checklist and have come up with your additional scope of work. You put your budget together for this property, and you determined that you are ready to purchase.

The first step is to get this property under contract. You need to lock it up. If this is your first time working with a wholesaler, they will require you to put a deposit down on the property purchase.

Depending on the type of area, the price range, and the current market, that deposit may be $500 or $1,000. If you are in a high-priced market with lots of competition and there is a Realtor or really old-school broker involved, they may ask for a lot more.

Be very wary about where you send this money. Your deposit should only go directly into the closing agent's escrow account. Ideally, that will be your title company or your real estate attorney. While arguably not appropriate, some sellers will demand that things go through their attorney or title company (like the government when buying HUD homes).

The better wholesalers will save you time by sending you an already prepared document that you sign to take over an existing assignable agreement, or if they own the property, they will send you a standard purchase and sales agreement.

QUICK TIP: The better you get to know your most common local real estate contracts, the faster and safer you'll be able to move through deals. Some new investors try to use all types of crazy contracts they found online or bought from some program. While you can technically make a binding contract with a few lines on the back of a napkin, most law offices and Realtors will require you to use their state bar or Realtor association contract. Get to know those by heart, and life will be much easier and less risky. You will make fewer mistakes and will become able to knock out a contract, on the spot, in just a few minutes.

That is where all the real work starts. If you find your own deals, you might think that is the big culmination of all your work. It's not. It's just the beginning. Plenty of deals fall apart for a wide variety of reasons. Managing the transaction and holding it together will greatly determine whether you are on top of or a flop in the real estate flipping game.

Take that purchase agreement or contract that you sign and send it over to your favorite title company with which you want to close. Notify them of the expected closing date, all the parties' contact information, how you will take and hold title, and if you need a survey or flood certificate. Let them know if you need a lender's policy in addition to your buyer's policy. If there is a lender involved, that will be mandatory. Let the title company know what type of loan you will be using. If it's a hard money lender, let the title company know to allow more time. Even with hard money lenders, there can be quirks.

You need to stay in constant contact with your lenders throughout this process. That begins with running your scenario by them and then making an actual application and sending them your contract. If you make sure they're available to be in contact with you and they have the funds available for you, you will be able to close the transaction on time.

With private lenders, the money should already be in escrow or in the bank. If the loan is being funded with a self-directed IRA, there is a rigorous process involved. You may need to add an extra couple of weeks to get those types of funds to the title company.

Staying in communication with all sides of the transaction before closing is very important. Talk to your lender. Talk to the seller. Talk to Realtors. Talk to your title company. Crazy things happen when you don't stay in constant contact with all of them. Just don't contact them so much that they can't make any progress on your deal.

On cash transactions, you can typically close in less than two weeks. Some can close in as little as 48 hours, but that only happens if you have absolutely everything together in advance.

Your attorney should be ready with any additional contracts needed to get approved for your private money loans. Other lenders will send their closing documents directly to the closing agent (your title company or law firm). You will sign final copies of everything at the closing.

VIP TIP: Read the fine print. It may seem silly, and you may be in a rush, but there is a reason some things are hidden in tiny print among lots of pages. No matter how much stress you are under, do not sign anything that is not completely true and accurate. There are severe criminal penalties for lying in real estate transactions. Being too lazy to read the fine print is not a valid defense if there is a problem with the contract.

Preparing for the Closing

Before closing, you must arrange for all the utilities to be connected in your LLC name, effective as of the day of closing. Some investors get into trouble when their house closes but the utilities have not yet been connected. There can be quirks in this process that you need to clear up in advance. Some utilities are tough to deal with, while others are very easy and efficient.

If you don't have power and water when you close, then having contractors come to work on the property is just a big waste of time and money. Even worse, you'll look like a complete amateur and lose credibility in the industry. Every day matters. Every hour is costing you money. You may even have appliances and systems at the property that you haven't tested or don't know the condition of because no utilities were connected during the initial inspection. Even if the property renovations don't start for two weeks after closing, get in the habit of connecting and transferring all the utilities upon closing to get it out of the way.

Access to the property is also important. Your people need to be able to get inside the property. You should absolutely be demanding your right to a final walk-through of the property the day before closing. Anything could have happened since you went under contract, so if you can't personally do the final pre-closing walk-through, then have someone you trust to handle it. You normally don't get keys to the property until the closing. If the house is vacant, you may get them earlier or they should already be in a lockbox. You want to avoid those "oh, just go break in" situations, which can really be risky.

Changing locks on day one is smart. Construction sites are very attractive targets for criminals and curious neighbors. You do want to have your own lockbox on the property for easy access to your property. You don't want to be carrying around hundreds of keys everywhere you go for access.

I like to put lockboxes on the back door of the property. That way, it's not clearly visible that the property is vacant. Lockboxes are important because they save you the time and the inconvenience of going to the property and meeting the contractors to let them in the house, especially when you have contractors that you know, like, and trust. Just let them get to work. Don't be another choke point in your own system.

I usually hire a local landscape company to maintain the lawn for the duration of the time I own the property. I always search out local companies, and I try not to stick with just one. The local ones will generally get you the best rate, and they show up more consistently. When you use one landscape company and they have to travel 45 minutes or an hour out of their way to cut one of your properties, the time constraints for that contractor generally mean your property is the first one not to get serviced if they are behind in their work.

In general, there is great value in giving as much business to the same vendor as possible. However, you don't want the lawn out of control on the day you start showing the property for resale or when you are having photos taken for the listing. Be loyal, but insulate your business with diversification in vendors. The same applies to lenders, title companies, Realtors, subcontractors, wholesalers, and so on.

Finally, when preparing to close, don't only ensure that you have all the liquid funds to close on time, but be sure your ID is good, too. Some deals may require a government issued photo ID that is valid for at least six months after the closing date. You don't want to blow your best deal because you forgot to renew your driver's license on time and can't sign the closing papers, either as the buyer or the seller.

QUICK TIP: If your closing costs (and cash to close) end up being higher than expected (which always happens) and cash is tight, you can ask your title company to help by working with prorations for property taxes in the escrow agreement.

Chapter 7

YOU'RE IN THE MONEY BUSINESS!

 When you start rehabbing, whether one or multiple properties at a time, you may think that you are in the construction business. Instead, you are really in the money business.

Money is what makes things happen. Money is what drives your business. Money is a significant reason why you are rehabbing. As CEO (or whatever you choose for your job title), your job isn't really working the rehab. You real job is managing the money. That is true in every business.

Your first and primary responsibility is to ensure you don't run out of money. Running out of money is the most common reason that businesses fail. Your second responsibility is to manage that money well. To get the best returns on your flips, you can and will use capital as efficiently as possible.

That may not sound like a big priority when you are starting up your real estate flipping business. If and when you take on partners, lenders, or shareholders, it becomes a legal responsibility called a fiduciary duty. Whether you seek public or private financing, decide to go public, or elect to sell your business, your company will be worth far more (and will be far more attractive to potential lenders, investors, and buyers) if you can maintain good accounting practices and smart money management. That could mean billions of dollars in value one day if you can keep your accounting diligently organized.

It's very easy to get a property and then let it sit for weeks before you get started on the rehab. That is one of the worst things you can do in the rehab business because time is money. In rehabbing, time is very much connected to the money you will make or lose on the property.

There are local, national, and global real estate cycles. There is the interest that you're paying for any financing on the property. You are paying for insurance coverages. You are for paying for utilities on the property. You are paying for yard maintenance. You are paying for all the construction going on before the property sells to the new buyer. You are not getting paid until a new buyer takes title to the property upon closing and your account gets funded with the proceeds from that property.

That doesn't even begin to account for the added risk of tornados, squatters, vandalism, theft, or freak accidents that can cost you a lot of money. That also doesn't account for any money you've put in as a down payment or for lender points and insurance premiums or for doing your due diligence (inspections and appraisals). Every day is an opportunity to make good returns on that money or to detract from the days you are making progress. A week is a long time in a rehab project.

Your number-one focus for the rehab is keeping up momentum and keeping your contractors working. The more systemized you are about rehabbing your property, the more clarity you will have. That will make hiring the right contractors and creating a successful outcome more likely to occur.

It does not mean you should rush the rehab and do a poor job. Organizing your contractors so they aren't working in each other's way or ruining work already done will avoid costing you more money in doubling work and materials.

In general, my rehab to retail projects range anywhere from two weeks to two and a half months to complete. Taking six months or more is just not wise. To keep our projects moving well, we have a few well-defined phases for how we work through the construction project.

Before reviewing those phases, remember that your primary job is not just managing the rehab. More importantly, your primary job is managing the money. As you grow, you should be spending more and more time on efficiently raising money, optimizing your processes for profitability, and managing inbound dollars more effectively.

Chapter 8

REHABBING PROPERTIES

Here is the process we use for renovating properties systematically and efficiently.

Nine Steps for Rehabbing Houses

Step 1: Clean-Out and Demolition

Step one is clean-out and demolition.

There are some junk hauling services that may work for you, or you can just rent a dumpster. At this stage, anything that needs to go in the dumpster needs to be put there. Don't prolong completing this phase. Don't leave your property looking like it is under construction or messy. That will attract criminals, bother the neighbors (your future clients), and detract from the value if you get any early showings.

NOTE: Remember that the neighbors around your investment property are going to be some of your prime prospects. They are going to watch your work, the quality of your rehab, how you handle the project, and how your contractors behave. That experience will either ruin your reputation based on how they talk with others about your business or make them want to sell to you and buy from you.

So remove everything from the property that is included in your scope of work. That may include ripping out the kitchen cabinets, tubs, shower surrounds, drywall, appliances, and landscaping. The end result of this phase is a nice, clean-swept location that becomes a blank slate to work in and on. Your clean-out and demolition should be so good that, even at this point, you've already added a lot of value to the property, and it could already be resold at a profit as a wholetail or prehab deal.

Step 2: Mechanical Items

This step is where you dig into all the mechanical and structural elements in and on the property to make sure those elements are sound. You don't want to start polishing things up and then have to rip them out because the mechanical or structural elements behind the walls aren't right. Any major items such as foundations, roofs, and pest infestations will probably be tackled during this phase.

More commonly, you will be working with the mechanics of electrical and plumbing systems. Essential to this can be replacing the main electrical panel, especially if the system hasn't been updated to ground-fault circuit interrupter (GFCI) electrical devices. The electrical system needs to be safe for the new owners, up to code, and able to handle today's appliances. Faulty wiring could be a fire hazard and should be found and corrected. Make sure there is a dedicated refrigerator circuit and a dedicated bathroom GCFI. Be sure to add the correct electrical components for any additional lighting fixtures that need to be installed.

The plumbing system also needs to be checked. Watch for any leaks, and correct any potential plumbing system problems before putting the house back together. We typically install new mixing valves in the bathroom and new shut-off valves at all vanity and sink locations. There are times when that may also be done at the location of the refrigerator.

NOTE: At this point, we do not replace any receptacles, switches, or finish trim. Make sure you keep all the parts for any plumbing kits, bath fans, or other rehab materials brought into the house in a safe location. That way, you can avoid having to repurchase new kits for shower trim, faucets, fans, or other finish parts because someone carries them away in what they thought was an empty box or throws them into the garbage by mistake.

Rural properties with their own wells and septic systems may need extra evaluation and attention. With septic systems that have been left for a long time, there may be roots to kill with a dose of copper sulfate. Water pumps need to be working properly, and if the house has been vacant for a long time, testing the water quality will give you and your potential buyers peace of mind when reselling.

Step 3: Creating the New Canvas

In this step, we are prepping the walls to become the new canvas for the home. This phase involves drywall repair and patching or texturing any rooms that may need it. You will need a good quality drywall contractor for this step. They can make or break the finish level of your property.

I've had lousy contractors that have made a mess out of a small repair. I have had great contractors that can take a house that is destroyed with holes in the walls and do spot repairs with drywall patches. They skim and finish the walls so precisely that you can't tell where the patches were made. In my opinion, it's well worth paying a little more for the right contractor in this step. The last thing you want is to incur lost time and the additional cost of replacing and refinishing whole sections of drywall because of sloppy work. Not paying for the right contractor will be much more expensive and time-consuming.

Step 4: Flooring

When it comes to flooring, we either refinish existing floors or install new flooring. If the floors are all solid oak and in great shape, we will sand and refinish or scuff and reclear them.

In the kitchen and bathroom, we use a 12" x 24" groutable stick tile. That may sound like a cheap shortcut, but I have actually found that new materials with a quality installation are as good as tile. I have also found that stick tile is not cold on your feet and even a little bit more comfortable.

Step 5: Trim

You will need to repair or replace any trim that is needed. In most cases, you will have to install new quarter round throughout the house. Whether you install new flooring or you do a full sand and refinish, you will need to install new quarter round because the old trim usually gets destroyed in the prior phases. Anywhere you have a bed trim, replace it with matching trim casing and base. Sometimes, all the trim is destroyed or the scope of the rehab work allows you to retrim the entire house and install new doors.

Step 6: Prepping for Paint

Prepping for paint is done by caulking to fill any repair marks, small damage to doors, or small holes in the trim. After those blemishes are filled with caulk, sand them until smooth.

Step 7: Painting

Next, paint the entire interior of the property. Use flat white paint on all the ceilings. Spray any existing trim that has oil varnish and clear coat on it with an oil-based primer.

After the primer is dry, paint all trim with semi-gloss white paint. Coat the interiors of all closets with white paint. We use earth tone colors on our walls, including light gray, navy blue, or light green. We paint all walls with a flat sheen.

Some color is okay, but as you have no doubt heard, the key to reselling is to keep everything as neutral as possible. It doesn't matter how fantastic a designer you are or how trendy you think a bold color may be, there will be buyers who have other tastes. You want the maximum number of buyers to love the property and envision their belongings there. Earth tone colors will also make spaces in the house feel larger.

Step 8: Finishes

Next, work to put all the final finishes back in the house. Install new outlets, switches, and cover plates. If the house had no existing grounding going to the outlets, run a two-prong outlet to match what was existing. If there is existing grounding, then install modern, three-prong receptacles that are up to code.

For lighting, we generally install LED lights on the main floors and pull-chain fixtures with LED lights in the basement. We use modern dome-style lights in all the bedrooms, sleek flush mount LED lights in the kitchen, and usually a chandelier with a modern touch in the family room.

We install a tile surround in the bathroom. Sometimes, we add a tile backsplash in the kitchen. We install all cabinets, and if we put granite in the property, we immediately call for granite templating.

Install all the finishing plumbing fixtures, including the shower trim, a bathroom vanity, a new toilet, and a new supply line to the connection in the kitchen for the kitchen sink.

Step 9: Equipping and Polishing

Next, have new appliances delivered and installed in the kitchen. Complete any landscaping on the exterior of the property. Cut and clean the yard and make everything crisp and ready for showings. The final clean-out of the house includes the windows being cleaned, the baseboards being wiped, the floors being swept or vacuumed, the inside of all cabinets and drawers being vacuumed, and all cabinet faces being wiped clean. Now it looks flawless, and buyers will notice that you did (or didn't) pay careful attention to those details.

Chapter 9

REMARKETING AND SELLING THE PROPERTY (AKA THE EXIT)

Staging the Property

Now you have a market-ready, empty home. You are ready to start marketing it for resale.

Many real estate investors have strong opposing opinions on when to begin marketing a property. Some are bullish on beginning some form of marketing the day you close on the buy side. They don't want to waste a day getting the property to market. There are cases in which someone will come along and see the potential, prefer to do their own finishes, and buy the property as is. Even if you aren't marketing, you may get people stopping by to try to get a peek at what you are doing or to make an offer. Don't automatically dismiss them with an it's-not-finished-yet response. That is a critical mistake that can discourage some new investors. Do the math on their offer versus any extra profit you will realize by waiting longer to complete the project.

For example, you buy a property for $50,000 at an auction and begin your demo. A local buyer walks onto your job site and is willing to contract today for $90,000. You could hold out to complete the rest of your planned scope of work, stage the property, and begin listing it through your regular channels, all of which will require you to put another $30,000 into the house. Once it's listed, you reach out to that earlier buyer and ask for $125,000 (a little above market and close to new construction in the area). If the buyer accepts that asking price, you've gained only $5,000 over the original offer because you put in another $30,000 but you are reselling it for $35,000 more.

In addition, you will be paying closing costs (and commissions, if you have a Realtor involved) on the higher exit price, which could eat up any gains from finishing the rehab at that sales price. More than likely, the earlier buyer will scoff at the new asking price anyway because they wanted to buy it at a good value with room for the property to appreciate over time and with the ability to choose their own floor coverings, wall colors, and appliances. You may have just flushed away $30,000, and weeks of time from your life by not accepting the original offer.

Know when to stick to the system and when to roll with common sense.

Many investors don't want to do any marketing until the property is 100 percent complete and polished. They want to ensure that their first impression in the market is a great one, the property shows flawlessly, it really looks amazing, and clearly has the value. I'm typically in this second camp. There is nothing wrong, however, with your agent putting feelers out to those in their database and on their waiting list to buy a home in order to let those prospects know your property is available. Certainly entertain any offers you get. That will be even more important when you are newer at flipping real estate or if you may be dealing with a longer rehab time that spans a change in season.

Assuming we have not already received a great offer and all the finishes and polishing have been completed, we will stage the house next to prepare to show and sell the property.

Start with some artwork on the walls. In the master bedroom, we install a king size bed and a small dresser. The dining room gets a table. The living room gets a sectional. We'll add some other furnishings throughout the house, depending on size, layout, and so on.

You can hire a professional contractor to do the staging. There are more and more of them to choose from. They will always proclaim the value of staging a home when trying to sell it. Generally, though, it is cost prohibitive to hire a company to do this for you.

We typically keep the same inventory of accessories and furniture and then rotate it through the houses we are selling. I have one of our in-house laborers move the staging inventory from house to house as our projects are completed and then sold.

We often stage just to take the photos we will use on MLS and then move the furniture to other projects if we have lots of deals coming through the pipeline.

Photos are extremely important. No photos equal no sale. Buyers can filter their online searches by seeking listings with more photos or listings that have video tours. Buyers are going to see hundreds of competing homes in the same price range within moments of going online, and they don't have time to look at all of them in person. Buyers typically will short-list several properties by the pictures they see and then short-list further to a couple of those properties they want to visit personally. So despite all the time and money you have put into rehabbing the property, a sale can often come down to a few seconds online to view those staged photos.

You can probably take acceptable and high-quality images for this purpose with just your mobile phone. You need not spend tens of thousands of dollars on camera and video equipment or drones and then get distracted spending your time and energy trying to become a master photographer and digital graphics expert. Remember to stay focused on your highest value activities.

Many Realtors will include professional photography with their services. Let them cover that cost. They probably have a much better deal on it thanks to their volume. Make sure you first clean up and polish the property. Make sure those listing photos are great photos. When you go online, you see all kinds of craziness. There are rehabbed houses where the photographer captures all the junk piled up in the bathtub or the unflushed toilet with the seat left up after being used. You invested tens of thousands of dollars to get to this moment, so don't let the failure to get great photos of a cleaned and polished room destroy so much value.

Listing the Property for Sale

There are a few paths you can take to resell your property.

- For sale by owner (FSBO)
- Full-service Realtor
- Discount realty services
- Flat fee MLS listings

The path of choice is really up to you. Do what is most profitable for you with the houses you are flipping. Focus on what you do best to create a well-oiled machine and efficient process.

FSBO

You can try to create your own resale marketing channels. Many investors today are trying to build their own websites, digital marketing funnels, and so on. That can be a useful option, but it can also require an investment of work, time, and funding to become a useful option. In the end, it may become a distraction from doing your more profitable skills and may not be very effective.

You can try to get noticed among all the sellers using online platforms such as Craigslist, advertising in local newspapers, and through other print or broadcast media.

You can also put for sale signs in the yard and on surrounding street corners and then sit at open houses every day until you sell. But statistics from the National Association of Realtors (NAR) show that only 7 percent of properties sell from yard signs and open houses. Those odds are pretty terrible and mean that this option will cost you time and money. There may be exceptions on certain streets with great visibility or when the market is white hot. If you can stick a sign in the yard and get multiple cash offers in a single day, that's great. If there is poor visibility or the homeowner's association won't allow signs, you're probably far better off pushing this option onto someone else or through an existing machine that makes it work.

Full-Service Realtors

Using Realtors may sound like an expensive venture, but that need not always be the case.

Some properties may really need a well-connected Realtor for resale. Examples are high-end luxury properties that may be targeted to an international group of very affluent buyers.

It's true that just like any other profession (including contractors and house flippers), only 1 percent may really be great at what they do. That can be frustrating at first, but it doesn't mean there aren't any good ones available or that the good ones you find don't have value. Let's hope the world doesn't write off the house flipping industry because of a few bad flippers, right?

In the beginning, a Realtor can be extremely helpful. It may be worth the investment on the first deal or two just to learn from them about the sell side. You will get exposed to the steps they take in a few days, based on their years of investment in education and experience, which is far more efficient than going to real estate school to get a real estate degree of your own. Realtors can bring a lot of value to your initial learning experience when investing in real estate. They can be a buffer in deal negotiation and legal liability. Licensed Realtors should carry insurance for errors and omissions that can protect you from being sued for simple mistakes in a real estate transaction. When it comes to picking Realtors, getting referrals from a trusted source or colleague who has worked with the referral is always best. Some Realtors love working with investors. Others don't.

Choose your Realtor wisely. Look for an agent with real experience. Real estate licensing courses don't teach much about doing business in real life. To learn this, Realtors need the experience of making transactions over several years. You should also look for an agent who is hungry and motivated. An agent who is too comfortable may be out of touch with the market and isn't going to hustle hard to take care of you and make your property sales a priority. Try to find an agent with some balance between hustle and experience. Despite all the hype, fancy ads, and slogans, all Realtors basically do the same marketing and get you on the same websites.

If you want to negotiate a great deal with a top agent, you can check out Realtor comparison sites such as Upnest. com where local agents will compete for your business and give you discounts. They can also compete to give you rebates if you are buying properties from MLS.

Discount Realty Services

Experienced agents should have the freedom to discount their service fees to win your business or to reward you for repeat business and loyalty. They can do so without doing less work for you and your sales.

There are some brokerages that advertise as discount agents but really won't save you much because they do a lot less work for you and your sales. Look for value, not just price.

Flat Fee MLS Services

Here's the big secret about the real estate industry and real estate agents.

The vast majority of properties in America are sold simply by putting them on MLS. It's not yard signs or open houses or postcards or flyers or Google ads or single home websites. It is MLS. Even Forsalebyowner.com admits that at least 80 percent of the five million or so homes sold every year in the United States sell thanks to MLS.

This is the Realtor's system for cataloging homes available for sale, publishing them online, and syndicating them on the Internet. So when you go to all the major real estate websites, you see the same homes. Your agent in Cleveland puts your home on MLS so buyers and agents all over the world will see it on Realtor.com, Zillow, Trulia, Redfin, and more.

Many Realtors will get your listing, lock in a 3 percent commission for themselves, throw it on MLS, and let another agent sell it to their clients and do all the real work.

MLS is your dream power tool as a seller. It is a machine that is already built, has mass with millions of views each day, and has qualified buyers with a sense of urgency looking at it right now. Use it.

There are a few ways to get your property listed on MLS. You can use a local real estate agent who knows the local market very well in your area. The agent will help you price the property, get listed on MLS, and generally take care of all the photography and more that's needed for the property.

My preferred method of selling is using a flat fee MLS listing service. For a nominal fee, they will post your property on MLS. That's really all they do. They may have some upsells and add-on options such as photography, signs, contracts, and so on. Otherwise, you'll be responsible for all those things. Their costs may not be competitive on those options because when you add the options, it may be more expensive than just going the full-service route in the first place.

Basically, the concept is that the flat fee service puts your property on MLS, and then a buyer (or a buyer's agent) will come to you directly. The process allows you to avoid incurring the listing agent's fees, although you are paying a flat fee for the service. This process also allows you to have more control over the contacts with buyers' agents because you are likely going to be paying the buyer's agent fees. You may pay $400 to get on MLS plus 3 percent of the sales price to the buyer's agent at closing, but you will pay no listing agent fees.

To really make this work, you have to be competitive in what you offer the buyer's agent. Being human and in a very competitive business, most agents are looking out for themselves first. That means they will cherry pick and be very selective in the listings they show their clients, often based on how much commission they will get paid on those listings.

Using a flat fee service, you get to pick the rates you are offering the buyer's agents. Some agents won't show these listings because they don't like innovative new services taking a bite out of their business. You could offer just 2 percent commission, but if a similar property is offering 4 percent, guess which property the agent is going to recommend to their client? The one, of course, that pays them more commission.

Another hack here is to offer bonuses and incentives. So you could offer 3 percent and then a 1 percent bonus if the house is under contract within two weeks and closes within four weeks. That motivates them to work to prioritize your sale. It's definitely worth it for you, too.

A flat fee MLS is my favorite service to use because I have flexibility to control what I need when flipping the property, especially when it comes to closing.

There is always seasonality in the local real estate market, along with swings in larger market trends. We most often like to launch our properties on a Thursday evening or Friday morning, ahead of the weekend competition. That way, we can be at the top of the list for buyers getting out to tour houses on Saturday and Sunday.

TIP: You'll never get the same attention and traction on the property as you do with the initial launch to MLS.

When MLS first lists your property, Realtors who are searching in the area will see it first in their search. Buyers and agents who have set up alerts on their phones and e-mails will get notified of it right away as a hot new listing. It is your one chance to really snag those serious buyers at the best price.

Thats requires you to have your property correctly priced at the moment you first launch it on MLS. If your price is too high and you get too few showings, you are going to lose opportunity, time, and money.

Watch your price brackets. For example, the agents of buyers qualified for a $100,000 home might search MLS for properties from $80,000 to $110,000. If you price your property at $111,500, you might miss all the right buyers because they will never see it. Likewise, those shopping to purchase from $111,000 and up won't see your property falling into the value level they are seeing in other homes closer to $150,000 and $200,000. Pricing is the number-one factor for selling homes at a good profit margin. If the property is priced right, it will sell and sell fast. If it isn't priced right, it will just sit and rot on the market.

There is only one factor more important than price for selling homes. That factor is follow-up. You can execute the perfect rehab, perfectly nail the pricing, and get lots of interest to buy, but if you are acting as your own seller's agent, you must be an ace at follow-up. So many sellers and real estate agents completely drop the follow-up ball. Many well-qualified homebuyers have given up on buying a home altogether, simply because sellers and agents don't reply promptly or don't reply at all. It's crazy, but it's true, and it happens after all the time and money that has been spent was put on the line to get to this point.

In sales, they say that after five minutes of an inquiry, your chances of closing the sale go down more than 90 percent. Those buyers are going to keep contacting the next home listing they like until someone answers and signs a deal. If you can't keep up with the inbound calls, texts, and e-mails, find an assistant. At the very least, find a remote or part-time assistant to respond and keep those buyers connected until you can get back to them yourself. Upwork.com can be a great way to pick from millions of virtual assistants and freelancers to help with these tasks.

If you don't believe someone is serious or qualified for this home yet (and you should never assume that they are), put them in a database so you can push out your next home that may be appropriate for them. This process will create a waiting list for your next rehabs.

Coordinating and Managing the Closing

Earlier in this book, I discussed how to choose the best possible buyer. The highest offer is not always what matters most. Instead, be sure you are looking closely at the details of the contract terms and the odds that the buyer can close on time.

Once you enter into a contract with your buyer, you are like the coach of a sports team. You are calling the plays and coordinating all your players to move in the right direction.

I prefer to deliver all the pre-closing documents to the title company as quickly as possible.

My typical closing overview starts with the buyer signing the contract. They are then allowed 10 days to conduct inspections. Any contingencies in their purchase agreement will generally be affected by those inspections. After the inspector goes through the property, it usually takes up to two days to get the report back. If the inspection discloses any issues with the property, the buyer usually asks for some concessions toward closing costs or the cost of the repairs to be made. You can agree, counter, or hold your ground. The loan process will stall until the contract contingencies have been satisfied. So we like to get the inspection out of the way and agree that the contingencies have been satisfied as quickly as we can.

Don't be the roadblock in your own closing. The pre-closing documents you will need to get to your title company may include the following:

- The signed contract or purchase agreement
- Your LLC operating agreement and certificate of status
- Contact information for whoever is holding the mortgage on your property
- Mortgage payoff letter and mortgage lien release
- Instructions for how you want to get paid

You can speed up the process by providing any recent survey and title insurance policy for the property. If you just closed on the buy side and your transaction hasn't been recorded or isn't showing up in public records online yet, make sure you can provide copies of your acquisition paperwork and deed with recording stamps to avoid any unnecessary delays.

When I use a private money or hard money lender to finance my deals, I promptly let them know the anticipated closing date, and I give them the title company's contact details.

When I was starting out in real estate, I was not contacting the title company and being proactive. I found that my failure to timely deliver our title documents and our mortgage lien release to the title company was holding up the closing on some of my properties. Typically, title companies are very busy, and they are managing a lot of closings. They don't always reach out to your lender in a timely fashion. They are going to push through the easiest deals, so we normally make the connections up front to build a proactive relationship with the title company. With time and volume, you will gain more weight and priority with the title company.

Your title and financial documentation aren't the only things that can hold up your closing. The buyer's lender can become a road block as well. Most of the time, their underwriting department will ask the buyer for more and more conditions to be satisfied and information to be provided before closing.

Some of these things can seem wild and unreasonable. Few can be argued with successfully. Keeping on top of your closings by making sure all the parties and their agents are cooperating with the title company and the lenders will greatly reduce the chance of having your closing delayed or totally collapsing. While most of the conditions will be requested from the buyer, make sure you immediately get and return any documents you are asked for so things can keep moving forward. You can expect that after those documents are delivered to the bank, it can take several days for them to be reviewed and approved.

When you are using private money or even your own money, it has a certain value to it—the time value of money.

Delayed closing dates can cost lost profits, lost or delayed opportunities on new deals, and extra finance costs or interest. Avoid closing delays as best as you are able.

Pre-Closing and Post-Closing Procedures

The more process-oriented your whole business is, the more smoothly and predictably things will work. There are many phases to a project and many factors involved in each of those phases. Don't expect you or your assistants and team to remember to check off all the boxes unless you've created boxes to check off.

Pre-Closing Process

The week of the closing, when we have confirmation that the bank has given a "clear to close" on the buyer side, we start putting our pre-closing process into action.

We call all the utility companies and give them an effective date of transfer when we are buying or a date to shut them off when we are selling. That is important. In the beginning, there were a few times we didn't call our utilities. It was overlooked, or we just counted on the new buyer to turn them on in their name. In one instance, in an area where I was not familiar with the water department, I paid the first three months of the new owner's water bill because the new owner never transferred the water service into their name.

That's not too big of a hit on its own, but when you multiply that by all your utilities across dozens of deals in a year, it all adds up fast.

In addition to your water, electric, and (maybe) cable, you should notify your lawn service company as well. Let them know what the transfer date is so they can discontinue services. Be sure to document those requests because you never know when a company will try to sneak in an extra month of service on your account.

Be sure to obtain releases for any mechanic's liens from contractors in advance of the closing. You don't want to be paying them twice out of your proceeds.

My golden rule is that regardless of whether you have a big enough team to handle it (or even if you're just a solo entrepreneur running the entire show), on the day before the closing, walk the property yourself prior to your client's walk-through appointment. If you can't walk the property yourself, have somebody you trust who has a very good eye for detail to do it for you. Make sure nothing on the property has changed. If there is an easy issue to solve prior to their walk-through, just get it done. Things happen.

By the time you are closing on the exit side, your property may have been unattended for several weeks. You never know what you might find during that walk-through. Someone could have stolen the appliances or, worse, the AC unit, and they may have stripped all the copper from the walls. A leak could have flooded the floors. Melting ice could have revealed a new leak. A tree could have gone through a window. Your Realtor could be camping out there, or you could have a crazed squatter living in the property. Someone could have run off with your lockbox and keys. You don't know if you don't check. A brief 10- to 15 minute walk-through of the property is well worth the assurance of knowing you are going to close without any headaches.

When you're investing, you don't get paid until after the closing happens and the money clears in your account. Even then, there can be questions. You will continue paying interest until you can transfer funds to pay off your lenders.

Even if you're not paying interest on that money, there is an associated cost to having those funds tied up in this deal.

Post-Closing Process

Some key things to think about after the closing include:

- Verifying the financials
- Storing the documents
- Canceling the insurance
- Managing your profits

Closings can make your head spin. They make you so dizzy with numbers and fine print that you can easily miss something. The number of line item costs on your first couple of deals can be absolutely bewildering. Signing stacks of documents can be truly exhausting. You may have been in a rush then, but someone should look it over again immediately post-closing to quickly catch any errors.

One of the top issues is ensuring all mortgages are paid off and all liens are released, with all these things being reflected accurately on the closing statement. Let's say the closing documents don't include paying off a specific mortgage. Since investors won't see the mortgage amount listed, they put an inadequate amount of money in the bank because the new owner still has that lien against the property. Maybe the title company didn't even pay the lender. Even if that is all worked out, if the closing documents aren't accurate, the IRS is going to determine that you received more money in your pocket than was actually paid to you. At the end of the year, that might look like you made an extra $1 million in income, and you will love getting that tax bill. Good luck if the title company goes out of business before you can fix those inaccurate closing documents.

Make sure you can prove your track record of successful and timely closings to future investors and private money lenders by storing all of your documents securely. Don't just store them on your computer, because you will lose them when your computer crashes. Scan the documents, and keep them on external hard drives and on the cloud. Preferably, have backups stored in more than one location such as Google Drive and Dropbox. You can save a local copy on your computer and external hard drives, along with the hard paper copies in a secure and fire-resistant file cabinet.

Be sure to evaluate your deals on a regular basis, at least monthly. You may want to do that alone or with your team to get their input. What went well? What did you do right? What could you have done better? How could you have done this faster, easier, more profitably, and with fewer mistakes? How can you remove more of yourself from the processes involved with technology and by hiring or partnering with others?

Maybe you can't see these answers from your own perspective. Ask your team, your vendors, and the other parties involved. Make sure they are comfortable enough to be truthful with you, even if they know you won't like the answer such as, "If you would just let us do our jobs, it would have been done better and in half the time." You don't have to act on every criticism or recommendation. Acknowledge them and collect them. If you see trends in these answers over months and multiple deals, then (whether you like it or not) these answers may be right. It may be worth testing their ideas just to see. The last thing you want is your own business to fail because you thought you knew better than everyone else.

Now, you get paid! Awesome, right? Well, what you do with those profits will directly influence how well you do going forward. One of the greatest traps of being able to make great money in real estate is a mindset or an ego that makes you think you have developed the Midas touch. You just made $50,000 in just a few hours work. That is more than most people make in an entire year working more than 2,000 hours. Don't blow it all by celebrating or buying something that will require being fed more money (like a new car). You can go bankrupt fast even if you're making a million dollars a year if you spend poorly and allow your bills to exceed your income. Rather, you can ensure that you keep going and multiply your success by investing that payday back into your business.

Do celebrate. Anchor this moment of success. Take your family or your team out for dinner. Buy a new outfit or write a big check to a local charity. Then put your money into buckets. That is far easier if you plan to do so in advance rather than starting to spend and hoping you have something left to reinvest in your business.

The savviest of businesspeople always say to pay yourself first. So, after any charitable contributions, you need to set aside any money you need for taxes and make sure you are saving something to invest in your education and in expanding your networks. Some of these things will be easier to cover if you allocate to those items a percentage of the profit from each deal since the numbers can vary so much after obviously paying off any debt with private money lenders, credit cards, store cards, lines of credit, and so on that you incurred to do each deal. Then decide how much you will be reinvesting in more deals for acquisition capital, rehab funds, and marketing funds. Don't forget that some of this money is also needed to carry your business and personal bills through to your next closing.

After all of these bases are covered, you've got some extra cash to spend as you see fit.

Chapter 10

SCALING YOUR FLIPS AND MAKING THE REAL MONEY

One of the biggest mistakes I see investors make when flipping to retail and with real estate in general is working on one project at a time. They are all in, working hard, day after day, trying to get that one deal done. The mistake they are making with this approach is that they are not focusing on lining up the next deal.

In reality, flipping one property every quarter is only going to earn you the kind of wages you could earn elsewhere working for a company. It may be an extremely great paycheck, but it's not going to make you rich, and you are taking on all the risk, stress, and accountability for making the deal profitable. This one-deal-at-a-time approach to real estate investment will not deliver on what got you into real estate unless you just need a hobby to keep you busy or a little extra spending cash to supplement your Social Security in retirement.

Keeping momentum, keeping pace, and having a consistent flow of projects will create more value and profits for your company. It will give you more of the results you really want from real estate investment, which includes but is not limited to more free time, less stress, the ability to control your own schedule, more truly disposable income, the ability to help others, a sense of fulfillment, and creating some real wealth and financial security that could provide a legacy you can pass down to your survivors, which will last long after you are gone.

If you are new to real estate investing, I do recommend mastering the art of completing one property and rolling right into your next one. Then get used to juggling a few at the same time.

If you wait until you've finished the rehab, marketed and sold the property, and gone through your post-closing checklist before you start looking for your next deal, it's going to be a really slow pace of investment. If you are picky about the deals you take on, there could be months between deals if you do one deal at a time. You may be doing only two deals each year if you follow this method—one deal in a good season and one deal in a tough season.

Using this method, your first deal of the year will have to carry all your expenses for the next six months, maybe longer. It will be very hard to get ahead financially with that math.

Having consistent deal flow helps your bottom line and makes your cash flow consistent. That will open up your earnings and return potential, which will make everything else more profitable and effective.

If you are keeping your contractors, Realtors, lenders, title companies, and others busy on multiple projects, they will be more willing to work with you on any pricing and scheduling issues. You will gain a price and cost advantage in the marketplace. That allows you to pay more for a property than your competition will and still make more profit on the deal.

To make real money in this business, you need to do multiple flips every month. Done well, that doesn't mean you have to work any harder in the process. In the beginning, it may be a little chaotic getting organized and into a good pace, but you can do it with practice.

Investing in multiple deals at the same time also helps minimize risk by spreading your eggs among multiple baskets. If all you have is one project, almost anything can happen to throw a wrench in your projections. A contractor runs off with your money, someone steals your materials, the house on each side of you sells for pennies at foreclosure, or a tornado takes the roof off the day you complete all your finishes before closing. It can happen on any deal. You can get out of it alive, but maybe not with the numbers you expected.

If you have three projects working simultaneously and one ends up losing a few thousand dollars, one comes in right on your projections, and the third ends up being a windfall deal with even more profit and a faster sale, you'll be doing just great on balance.

When you are consistently closing properties one right after another for five to six months, you will be ready to scale your systems and operation. A single investor can easily work on three to four deals every month. There are some large investor groups doing volume of more than 100 or even 200 deals a year. I believe that you, as a single investor, can do at least three or four deals a month.

It may sound like a big leap to go from 10 properties a year to 30 or 40, but don't be intimidated.

Really, the only strategy difference in scaling up to three or four properties per month is working on your incoming deal flow. That is generally the bottleneck because you don't have good systems for getting deals on your desk to review every single day. If you have a truly good incoming deal flow, you'll be able to find the funding and buyers. If you have a good inbound flow of deals but you are not scaling up the number of deals you close monthly, then your bottlenecks are probably financing, contractors, or buyers. These scaling strategies will work if you find the right help and implement ways to work with them.

There are three skill strategies you will need to start scaling your real estate business.

1. Working with Contractors

Create good relationships with good contractors using systems that do quality work.

2. Raising Capital

Continually develop relationships with your capital sources and financing structures to eliminate constraints and delays.

3. Networking and Relationships

Find more wholesalers, sellers, buyers, and referral sources to increase your influx of good deals and conveyor belt process for exiting those deals by getting them out of the inventory and turned back into cash.

It's okay to start small. Trying to do too much at once will leave you feeling overwhelmed, so start where you can. Get good at the small things, just don't get lost being stuck there. Remember why you started on this path in the first place, and set a timeline to scale it up.

Do not sell yourself short. You have incredible potential. If you don't feel a duty to live at your full potential for the world or for anyone else, then do it for yourself. At the end of the day, you can say you gave it your all, you did your best, and you fulfilled your potential with purpose. If you can say that, the math doesn't really matter.

So think really big. How much money do you want to make, or how many people do you want to help with new homes? Can you help 100 people a year?

Then back out the math and tasks needed to make that happen. What processes and people will you need in order to achieve and operate on that level? Decide what the one most impactful thing is that you can do next toward scaling up. Do that one thing. Then identify and do the next. Keep repeating, and you'll be amazed where you are a year from now.

Be sure to drop me an e-mail and let me know about your progress. I love hearing success stories!

Chapter 11

THE 3 C'S

There are 3 C's to succeeding in rehabbing and flipping properties. Master them, and you'll have a great edge in consistently generating quick and profitable deals. If you don't, you will be losing time and money.

The 3 C's:

1. Contractors
2. Capital
3. Contacts

Contractors

Contractors are your best asset and biggest hurdle in your flip to retail real estate business.

Contractors will make or break you. If you don't have relationships established with great contractors you can count on, then it doesn't really matter if you can find all the deals in the world at pennies on the dollar, or if you have a great eye for design, or if you have 100,000 people on your list of waiting and qualified buyers. Those deals will never get rehabbed or resold at retail without great contractors to do the work.

If you have an awesome construction team, you can find mediocre deals at so-so prices and still move plenty of deals each month. You can relist them on MLS to find buyers for bigger profits than your competition is making.

You need a construction team comprised of the following:

- Qualified contractors who are capable of doing the work required
- Accessible contractors you can work with smoothly and efficiently
- Reliable contractors who can get the job done on time
- Affordable contracting help

The critical importance of developing an awesome construction team is something many investors overlook. So let's start with the differences between contractors. There are two types of contractors and contractor businesses.

The first type of contractor is a "retail contractor." These contractors typically work for residential homeowners or commercial companies. They have a very strong marketing and sales presence in the community. While this type of contractor may have a great business and may work well for regular homeowners and commercial companies, they probably are not the optimal choice for you as a rehabber because they are very busy. Retail contractors sometimes have hundreds and thousands of customers, many who have more money than you do. That won't work when you need your projects done on your schedule.

You also do not want to pay for the higher overhead expenses of a retail contractor, including extremely long warranties, marketing, branding, new work vehicles, and the like. When you pay a retail contractor, you're paying for all those things. Their marketing. Their sales team. Their receptionist answering phone calls, and so on. That is why you will see a price premium of 20 percent to 30 percent for retail contractors. There is nothing wrong with this model, but it is more expensive and typically will not give you much control or influence over your schedule on getting things done.

That is fine when you're a homeowner and plan to stay in your house for seven or more years. You want to have a great and long-lasting warranty backing the incredibly expensive installation of what you just invested in. As a homeowner, you can also wait months while the retail contractors hop between all their projects, making an appearance at each.

The fact is that you are paying retail contractors for a retail service. Although some of those companies can add value to your business, they generally are not going to be your best fit. You can't afford to pay full retail on the houses you buy because you are trying to get everything wholesale so you can make a profit by selling retail.

The second type of contractor is one that doesn't have a sales team. They are not a company focused on sales. They do not spend money on marketing. They do not offer large and long-lasting warranties. They may not even have a website, or at least not a fancy one. Most of them will honor their work and follow up with a warranty. I call the second type of contractor "producer contractors" because they get the work done. They show up, they repetitively do good quality work, and they get in and out of your job site quickly and efficiently.

Producer contractors will seek out builders, investors, and business owners to do work for. Their work ethic is their marketing. They are more like your wholesale contractors. Their truck may not be as pretty, but they have better prices.

Finding Contractors

When it comes to rehabbing, you will generally be focusing your attention on finding producer contractors. The next question people always ask me is this: "Where would you go about finding a contractor like this?"

Normally, we go to new construction sites or communities where multiple homes are being built and search out contractors with whom we can work. It is an opportunity to get a card from and make contact with a potential producer contractor. It is also a chance to see what their work quality and work ethic are really like. That's a far better indicator than any sales hype or fake online reviews.

Most producer contractors are very busy. They get a lot of calls to their cell phones and always have a full voicemail.

That is why I like face-to-face meetings. I won't just talk to one of the crewmembers. I will ask if the owner is on site and then seek out that owner to shake his or her hand. I use this contact to introduce myself and let the the contractor know I am a real investor who works on properties in the local area.

I usually ask them to save my number on their phone right there on the spot. That way, next time I call them, my name will pop up, and it's not a random number they don't recognize.

That gives you a much better chance of making contact. A lot of these contractors don't regularly check their voicemail. They are too busy. You are often leaving messages, and sometimes the voicemail is full.

The second part of hiring a new contractor is getting the first project underway with the contractor and starting your working relationship.

You will both be playing a dance on the first few projects. You're trying to get the work done at a cost that's reasonable. You want them to keep a clean site, not damage finished work from other trades, be nice to the neighbors, and keep materials from getting stolen.

Of course, this relationship is not just about you. You also have to look at it from the contractor's perspective. They haven't worked for you before, and they are still trying to feel you out. Here are their big concerns: Will this investor pay me? Will I be paid on time? What level of detail is required on this project? Their schedules can be wild because they often do not know what their workload will be for the next few weeks. All they know is that you want the work on your property done immediately. They may tell you they can get right to work on your property so they don't lose the work, but that's not helpful to you if they can't deliver.

For every poor contractor out there, there is an investor who has done contractors dirty, including an investor who hasn't paid, an investor who is always dragging their feet on paying, an investor who constantly makes excuses or complaints about the work so they can delay paying, or an investor who is generally a nightmare to work with, either because they don't know how to manage a project or they are too detailed and fussy. Your work is definitely cut out for you—to prove you are one of the few good investors and that this relationship is a good fit for the contractor.

Most problems in life and business are due to poor communication or a disconnect in expectations. I prefer to set my expectations with the contractor up front. I am very clear with them about how much detail to quality I expect and how I will pay them. That is extremely important, especially on the first project (or even the first five projects) with a new contractor. By then, they may know you better than you know yourself.

It's really simple. Whatever you say you're going to do, you do it. Do it exactly how you said you would do it. If you tell them that you are going to meet them on the site at 9:00 a.m. to go over a few details, then be there to meet them at 8:45 a.m. Be early, and beat them there. If you say you're going to provide a check for 25 percent of the job at that meeting, then be there and hand them a check for 25 percent of the project without them asking. That shows them that you are very serious and very committed. They can then focus on their job, not worrying how they will pay their bills. Better yet, when they see you continue to act that way, they will go above and beyond to keep your business.

SPECIAL NOTE: When you make payments to the contractor, always have a written contract for the work you are having the contractor do. Never exchange money without having that contract signed by both parties.

Second, let your contractor know that you require a lien release signed at the end of the project and that you'll be giving them a check upon completion as long as they signed the lien release. That is absolutely critical to protect yourself from any third-party liabilities or clouds on the title of your investment property. Go to **formsforflipping.com** to get a copy of our lien release.

A lien release is a document stating that your contractor has been paid in full for your project. It also states that the contractor cannot put a lien on your property for any work they have done on the property prior to the signing of the lien release. Legally, contractors can place a lien against your property to ensure they get paid. That way, if you fail to pay them, they will get paid when the property is sold, when it is refinanced, or when it goes into foreclosure (providing there is enough equity). That does not mean contractors are happy waiting that long. It is an emergency backup. The release form will also protect you at closing if the contractor, for some reason, made a faulty claim. Remember, they are crazy busy.

If a dispute arises over the payment to your contractor, the contractor can formally file a lien against your property or refuse to waive and release a lien. They told you a price and you accepted it, they finished the work, and now they want more money on this job for some reason. The contractor can go to the county where the property is located and file a mechanic's lien on that property. The mechanics lien is an encumbrance on the property, so when you complete your house rehab, you can't sell and close it without paying the contractor the additional funds to release the lien.

The title company will see the lien pop up when running a title search on the property. You will need to satisfy the lien in advance, or the title company will satisfy the lien upon closing the property by taking the money to pay it out of your proceeds.

The bottom line is that this extra bill will need to be paid prior to the closing, or you may have to delay closing to go to court to fight the lien. In both cases, it will tie up your money and your time to find a solution.

As real estate investors, we are not just in the business of contracting to repair and flip properties. We are in the business of money. That is why only working with people you know, like, and trust is a top priority at all times. After you have achieved a good working relationship with your contractors, you will also learn the strengths and weaknesses of each one. Then you will know which contractors are better to assign to certain projects.

You will have more options as you build a collection of contractors. Some of the more detail-oriented contractors will be perfect for certain flips you are working on. Some of them might be more focused on getting the work done more quickly and for a better value. There is room in your organization for all these contractors to have a place. Make sure that your best and most versatile contractors are kept busy at all times and are paid on time. You do not want to lose them once you find them, especially after you have developed a working relationship with them. So keep searching for deals to fill their project pipeline with bountiful work that targets their skill sets. Remember, good contractors are one of your most valuable assets.

Capital

A contractor's toolkit is comprised of all implements they have inside their truck, van, or trailer. They need to make sure they have air guns to drive nails, saws and sharp blades to cut wood, knives to cut drywall, and brushes to apply paint. They also need gas in their vehicles to get them to the job sites.

An investor's toolkit is comprised of a notepad, a pen, a smartphone, and capital needed to fund real estate investment deals.

Capital is money. Money is a tool. You can't do business without capital. Your capital doesn't always have to be all your own money, but you are going nowhere without any capital.

Don't believe me?

Imagine you secured funding for a property you purchased for $50,000. Then you have an estimated rehab budget of $20,000. You're now rolling three to four projects at a time. So all your cash is tied up in those projects.

Thankfully, you just closed on a property, and you have $20,000 for your rehab budget wired directly to you from the title company. You start the rehab, and then bam! You run into an issue. Now you need an additional $10,000 in your budget to finish the rehab. You are temporarily cash broke, even though you may have $1 million in properties. You hope to have $40,000 in two weeks from another closing, but that is a recipe for disaster. What if the other deal falls through? Or it doesn't close on time? Most won't.

Worse yet, you can't pay suppliers, contractors, or utility bills. Your cash flow could now potentially put a bottleneck in your project. Let's say you missed three small things on this property: (1) your furnace doesn't operate properly and must be repaired or replaced; (2) you discover a small water intrusion in the basement that was not seen during the pre-closing walk-through and requires repair; and (3) you discover some miscellaneous landscaping items in the yard that were not seen during the pre-closing walk-through. This may all total, let's say, $10,000 in additional repairs, which represents $10,000 less that you will get at closing. Within the next week, you need to get additional funding for the $10,000 or this project bottleneck is going to cost even more money. You have a recipe for disaster. You may have four rehabs going on at the same time, and you might have four to six other properties on the market, but if you are going over budget on multiple properties while some are not netting the proceeds you expected, you are in trouble.

If you can't fund all the little things that keep the engine running and the wheels turning, then your contractors are going to stop working. If the utilities are off, then the contractors can't do all their work and you can't properly show the property. If your cell phone gets cut off, you can't connect with anyone. Those scenarios can snowball like a row of dominos and get very ugly really fast. **You always have to have contingencies or extra funding to cover these sorts of issues.** Otherwise, production stops because you can't pay contractors, and you can't buy supplies. In addition, you will have recurring interest charges from your mortgage notes, and you will have insurance payments for your property and business.

You absolutely must have a plan for these unexpected occurrences. You might have a closing that you've been waiting on for a month or 45 days. That deal could fall through at the last minute, or the closing could be extended an additional month the week of closing. It's happened to me. I've learned the hard way by making those mistakes. I'm writing this book so you don't have to learn the hard way.

Earlier in my real estate career, I went to do a project with wide eyes, expecting to make a $30,000 to $40,000 return. That project went from a 90-day rehab-to-money in the bank to an eight-month money-intensive waste of time. That particular project, even with contingency money available, slowed me down on other deals for which I was going to make even larger returns.

My point is not that you need to have huge amounts of reserve funding. That certainly doesn't hurt, but going into a project and underestimating the rehab budget you need in order to make the deal work or thinking your initial rehab budget will be right on with no room for issues will always serve to put you into a losing deal. You need to plan for the unexpected because you must expect the unexpected.

Remember, the time to raise money and secure credit lines is not in the bottlenecks of cash-poor crunch times when you are desperate. No one wants to make a loan to you then. When you first start to raise money and secure credit lines, you should gain access to more funding than you need so you don't get crushed in these bottleneck situations. Don't make these mistakes so you aren't learning the hard way.

When working on raising capital and credit, you need skills such as organization, money management, credit management, and future funding projections. The easiest money and best terms are available when you don't really need it. Funding will be less available and really expensive if you are already running tight on cash.

The best way to raise capital is through a network of investors. In particular, you should seek out investors who want to be passive in the real estate market.

You can also back up your liquidity and emergency funding with the following:

- Personal and business lines of credit
- Secured credit lines on savings and CDs
- Working capital loans and cash advance facilities
- Home equity lines of credit (preferably not on your primary residence)
- Business credit cards
- Setting aside a percentage of each sale for reserves

Structuring your real estate deal with your investor is very important.

When working with investors, each one is going to be a little bit different. It is important to be able to offer them what is most important to them when negotiating for your funding, just as when you are negotiating with sellers and staging your home for buyers.

There are lots of ways to structure your investor-funded deals. One of the most common ways is to have an investor totally fund the property purchase. You give them a mortgage and promissory note to protect their interest in the property. It could be an interest-only note payable for a three- or six-month term. Personally, I don't recommend mortgaging a property for less than six months. Delays can and will happen. Markets can and will change. If your loan matures before you flip, you run the risk of the investor foreclosing on the property and losing your investment and your time.

Always get more time to repay your loans than you think you will need. If you need to refinance that deal in a short amount of time, it is going to become very expensive and can eat up your profit. If the property has been sitting on the market for some time or if unforeseen construction issues pop up, you can easily run over the deadline. At a minimum, you want your original loan agreements to include a guaranteed loan extension for another six months, providing you haven't missed any payments.

You might offer an annual interest rate of 8 percent to 12 percent on the loaned money that you invest in the deal. Those rates will vary over time depending on the market, conventional mortgage rates, available capital, and rates paid for competing and comparable investments.

To calculate the interest payment, take the entire amount of the loan and multiply it by the percentage rate. If it's 8 percent on a $50,000 note, multiply 50,000 by .08. That is going to be the amount of annual interest you owe (due for one year). Divide that amount of annual interest by 12, and that number is the monthly interest payment you will be making.

You can also use the free online mortgage calculator at mortgagecalculator.org, which allows you to propose all kinds of scenarios and structures to find the payments and pricing that work for you.

Some investors may want to see a return on their money of 8 percent to 10 percent **plus** a percentage of the deal profits after closing. If so, you should say, "Mr. Investor, I will give you your 8 percent to 10 percent **plus** a percentage of the deal profits after closing, **but** that is all going to be payable after closing." When working with investors, it's extremely important to be thorough, detailed, transparent, and confident. Remember, it is all about setting expectations. Capital investors aren't mind readers, so be clear, and leave room to overperform so you can WOW them.

Working with capital investors is like working with contractors because you must always do what you say you will do. That rule can never be broken.

Ready access to investment capital is a great asset to any real estate company, and it is the only way to be able to scale. That also comes with a heavy burden of responsibility to your capital investors because you are investing other people's hard-earned money, possibly their life savings, to make your deals.

You need to take that responsibility to your capital investors very seriously. There have been deals in which I have personally lost money, yet I still returned profits and the entire principal invested to the investor. That's just straightforward good business, even though it was done at my expense, because it kept my investor investing with my real estate business. The experienced and realistic investor will know that not everything will always go smoothly and according to plan. The difference is what you do when things do not go as planned. I always take my capital investors' money more seriously than I take my own, so I always make sure my capital investors get paid in full before I get paid.

If you do run into an issue or a snag, do not be afraid to reach out to your investor. It is important to keep lines of communication open. If a deal is not going to close on time, or if you ran into some problems with the house and need some additional funding, do not be afraid to go to your investors.

They may be willing to extend your loan, or they may be willing to find additional money to get the project finished, especially if they already have a mortgage on the property. They can add to the loan, provide a second mortgage, or just put up the cash as a personal loan. I would not make a habit of doing that, but if you get into a jam, these are viable options. You don't know if you don't ask. You should at least give them the opportunity to help save the deal. Then let them make their decision. No matter what happens, open communication is always the key to determining your options.

Contacts

Growth and success in the real estate investment industry is still all about who you know.

To be a successful flipper, who you know is far more important than what you know. Your success is directly tied to the number of people in your network, as well as the number of people who know you and your business.

That may not seem fair, but the good news is that networking is one of the great eveners of the real estate investment landscape. You can add to your contact list and expand your circle today and every day.

Making new contacts should be one of your top-priority tasks. Schedule time to make new contacts every week. It can be the most powerful thing you can do to help your business grow and succeed.

You may not have a dime to invest in real estate, or you may not know much about real estate and its different sectors, but if you know people who do, then your business can grow and succeed.

Your contacts should include the following:

- lenders
- investors
- sellers
- buyers
- renters
- contractors
- business professionals
- Realtors
- industry vendors

You contacts are worth more than their weight in gold. Your competition is probably paying an average of at least several hundred dollars per lead for their deals. Just one deal or loan from one of those contacts is easily worth more than an ounce of gold. Remember that each contact is a doorway to at least several hundred other new contacts.

Never dismiss your contacts or throw them away.

Ultimately, your contact list is going to be the most valuable part of your business. Companies such as Facebook and Google are worth so much money because they have the contact information for billions of people.

Build your contacts into a spreadsheet, or save them in a group in your phone contacts. Put them in the cloud, and upload them to your e-mail service so you can reach out to them easily in the future.

Among your contacts are the people you will constantly reach out to for new deals. They include real estate wholesalers, individual sellers who know your business, Realtors who can find you deals before they hit the market, probate attorneys, and so on.

Block out an hour once a week to communicate with the people in your contacts through varied methods. Let them know you are still there and still in business.

Do this with your family, too. People are busy. They don't always have time to figure out if you are still in business or learn about all the services and ways you can help. You must constantly remind them in order to keep your contact information at the top of their minds and at the tips of their fingers. Otherwise, when your mom tells you she sold her house for 50 cents on the dollar to one of your competitors, or your grandma refers her neighbor's heirs to sell their property to some random homebuyer who sent her a postcard, it is really going to spoil your day.

Ask your family members if they have any properties you can look at or if they need help with anything on their property. These people will serve you and your business, and you will serve them in their businesses and lives. That's a mutually beneficial relationship. All good business dealings I have been part of are mutually beneficial ones.

One day, you might help one of your contacts by putting them in touch with a contractor or an attorney you know. On the other hand, you may need the help of one of your contacts to find a person inside their circle and schedule an introduction.

One thing I've learned about contacts is that they never go dormant. People move and shift positions. They find new work avenues. You never know who your contact is going to know and who they may know in the future.

Never dismiss or underestimate people. Don't judge them by what they wear or by their first offer. Many of the wealthiest people walk around in hoodies and jeans, not overpriced suits. That geeky looking kid could be the next Mark Zuckerberg. That homeless looking lady could win the lottery.

I have contacts I've known since I was 18 years old. They are still relevant today. We are still in contact with each other. They don't work at the same company when we first met. They've moved on in their careers. And I don't work at the same company, either. We are all working to better ourselves, and sometimes that means moving to a new job or business venture.

Keep your contacts in your spreadsheet. Identify the most value-added contacts who seem to be creating the most deals for you. Then find a way to thank them with a special gift, a thank you letter, a meal at a restaurant, or a few hours at a sporting event.

Do that with your top five to 10 referral sources. Make an effort to reach out to them once every two weeks or at least once a month. That could create an opportunity to talk with them about the option of private lending. Unless you ask, you will never know if they may be able to or want to participate in capital lending. For people who have referred large numbers of properties to me, I will sometimes give them a larger ticket item as a thank you gift. People notice when you show your appreciation. It is always an easy and highly valuable thing to do.

Chapter 12

THE SILVER BULLET FOR SUCCESS

The Secret Formula for Success

Ready for the secret formula for success?

Here it is. Here's the silver bullet—that magical moment and golden nugget you have been waiting for throughout this whole entire book.

Are you ready for it?

Go to the next page.

Sorry, there is no silver bullet.

There is no magical hack or shortcut to overnight success.

Work the System

Success comes incrementally through the accumulation of the small daily wins you achieve by taking the actions you committed to take. Overnight success is what happens after you keep hustling and consistently doing the small things right over a long period of time.

Every time you help a seller get out of a sticky situation, that's a win. Every time you help one of your investors get a good return on their money, that's a win. Every time you revive and improve a house, that's a win. Every time you provide a paycheck to your contractors, that's a win. Every time you sell a great new home to someone, that's a win. Keep chocking up those wins, and the money will take care of itself.

To get there, invest in yourself and your mindset. Create value for others. Hustle to get things rolling. Keep hustling to get things done on time. Always look to maximize your limited and valuable time. Plan for the unexpected things that will arise. Master your 3 C's (contractors, capital, and contacts).

Stay focused.

Real estate is a very complex business and a very simple business, all at the same time. It's complex because there's a lot of moving parts, but with organization, it is a very repetitive and predictable process. When broken down, each part can be very simple, even to sending out multiple offers on houses each day.

You will not always be guaranteed a predictable outcome, but the process itself can be created to become predictable. You can move the odds in your favor, especially with scale.

Find What You Are Passionate About

I build value in my companies with my strengths, and I try to find people to do the jobs I am weak at.

Early in my real estate investing career, I tried to assume all the roles and responsibilities of my company. When I was weak in any specific area, I always tried to compensate or make myself better in that area. There is always continual improvement you can make, but I don't think you should be focusing a lot of your time and energy on trying to improve on weaknesses that are not something you want to be doing or aren't passionate about.

Passion is what drives success. Passion will keep you moving. Passion will inspire others to come with you on your journey. If you take a job you are not passionate about, you will never have long-term success. I read about this concept in books when I was in my teens and 20s, but it wasn't until my late 20s (when I was operating another company I founded) that I really began to appreciate the importance of passion in my work.

The outcome I ultimately became passionate about was bringing a new service to the company. We had just finished a one-off project, one for which we were forced to provide this rehab service, and it proved to be very lucrative. I immediately went back to my office where I sat down and thought, "How can I make this service something we spend more time doing? How can I make this service the only thing we do?"

I had that passion and drive, and those types of jobs started attracting me like a magnet. I wasn't even marketing that heavily for these projects yet, but soon my team and I were doing 25 percent of our business in that category. I thought it was amazing. I loved it, and I loved the feedback our clients were giving us. We excelled in this category because we didn't set out to be just average flippers. Instead, we set out to be the best flippers. I have applied this high standard to every new project and business we undertake. Find out what you are most passionate about, and excel at it.

When I started in real estate, I used the same concept. Real estate was something I was already passionate about, and I am extremely passionate about the types of real estate transactions we're doing now. We're taking distressed, ugly, outdated properties and adding value by modernizing them. At the end of the day, we are creating something to show for our actions, and we are profitable. That is the lifeblood of any successful business.

Taking Inventory

Whether you are already very active in real estate or have just done a few deals but are struggling to get real growth and profitability, it's always smart to invest some time and take an inventory of your work.

That means taking a moment to sit back and look at your numbers. You can take a day off to do this from home, go into the office on a weekend and do it, or even go check into a hotel somewhere to get focused and avoid distractions. Sometimes, the farther away you get, the more clarity you can gain from having a different perspective.

Look at the profitability of your jobs. Look at the real numbers. If you're fudging numbers and lying to yourself about where money is on a job, you are only hurting yourself. You must pull actual data on what the job costs and how much you really made from your last three to seven flips.

Figure out which one to three flips were the most profitable and which ones you lost money on. Figure out why you lost money on those jobs and write it down. Don't buy properties where you will again lose money, because it's very easy to need another deal but buy the wrong property. In this business, your properties need to coincide with the niche category upon which you are ultra-focused. That is how you gain clarity of your purpose. That is how you own space in your markets. That is how you create success in your flips.

Dig into those deals and do not just set refined criteria for properties you will and will not buy. Look at the rehab project and what worked and what didn't. Look at your resale process and what worked and what didn't. Look at your financial structuring and see where you can create more profitability, minimize more risk, and make better deals.

After you have taken inventory, go back to your team and get them on board with your new focus.

Flipping through the Fear

For those of you who have not yet done your first flip, the awesome news is that you are just one transaction away from doing that first flip. Get out there. Get your first property under contract. Do whatever you've got to do to get the first flip done.

Then you can evaluate the process of your first transaction from start to finish. Decide what you loved to do on the transaction, what you excelled at, what went well, and where you can improve for the next flip. Then purchase your next property. Rinse and repeat.

Fear is normal. I don't care what big business leader, billionaire entrepreneur, or real estate mogul you name, admire, and think is so confident. Each and every one of them has felt fear. I guarantee it. They have been terrified. They couldn't sleep at night. They doubted themselves. Good thing they kept going, right?

There is no shortage of excuses for those who just want to cuddle up under the blankets with their fear and hibernate through life. However, what I really want is for you to succeed. There are so many opportunities out there that no single investor or billion-dollar fund can handle them all.

What you should be truly afraid of is not taking action. If you don't take action to change things now, it will never be easier to get started. It will only get harder and harder to take that first step. If you keep doing what you are doing, you will keep getting the results you are targeting. Life is meant for being GREAT, not just for being good.

You can do it!

Chapter 13

WHAT'S NEXT?

Congratulations on finishing this book!

You have already made a great investment in yourself. I can't wait to see what you do with this information.

We have considered many of the mistakes I've made, so hopefully you won't have to repeat them. We have touched on some of the tools you can use to keep learning and growing. We have touched on goal-setting, various types of real estate investing strategies you can try, and why I love rehabbing to retail so much.

I've given you my step-by-step process for getting started and flipping your first deal, as well as how to structure and plan your rehab projects with a strong system. Hopefully, you have gained some great insights about staging and marketing your properties for a fast and profitable resale, as well as for mastering those 3 C's.

So, what's the next step?

I've included some additional resources where you can get more information and tools to develop your real estate investment business.

Maybe your next step is making that first offer and doing your first deal. Maybe your next step is taking a moment to evaluate your deals and create a more profitable system. Maybe your next step is making that commitment to scale your business and take it to the next level. Maybe your next step is finding a mentor or coach to help you get that breakthrough.

What's your next move?

Don't hesitate. Do it!

ADDITIONAL RESOURCES

mikemireiter.com
formsforflipping.com

www.ingramcontent.com/pod-product-compliance
Lightning Source LLC
Chambersburg PA
CBHW060458280326
41933CB00014B/2784